# Where He Dwells

## READINGS FOR ADVENT

2023

CHRISSIE TOMLINSON

# Isaiah 25:9

*And it will be said in that day,*

*"Behold, this is our God*
*For Whom we have waited*
*That He might save us.*
*This is the Lord*
*For Whom we have waited;*
*Let us rejoice and be glad in His salvation."*

1

*Our wreaths and ribbons and colored lights, our giving of gifts, our parties with friends- these have never been ends in themselves. They are but small ways in which we repeat that sounding joy first proclaimed by angels in the skies near Bethlehem.*

*In view of such great tidings of love announced to us, and to all people, how can we not be moved to praise and celebration in this Christmas season?*
*As we decorate our tree, and as we feast and laugh and sing together, we are rehearsing our coming joy!*
*We are making ready to receive the one who has already, with open arms, received us!*
*We would prepare you room here in our hearts and*
*Here in our home Lord Christ.*
*Now we celebrate your first coming, Immanuel,*
*Even as we long for your return.*
*from "A Liturgy to Mark the Start of the Christmas Season"*

*Douglas McElvey*

# Introduction

## A BOOK ABOUT HEAVEN

This is a book about Advent and Christmas. It's also a book about Heaven, because that's what the season of Advent and Christmas is about- the Lord coming to earth to secure our redemption, and the promise we have that He will return for us soon. Most years, we miss the connection between Christmas and Heaven. We seem to want to keep it either in the past or in the here and now. Let's just keep it about the angels and the shepherds, the wisemen, the star, the sheep and the donkeys. Let's keep it on December 25 and keep Jesus in the manger on the coffee table. Let's keep it about the tree and the lights, the turkey and the candy canes. But without the glory of Heaven illuminating it all, it's just another holiday.

When we do make Advent about the truth of our coming King, we feel the tug from the Holy Spirit that urges us to come away from the busy, and when we do, we can hear Him guiding us through a season of preparation for Christ's return. Sometimes that preparation means He shows us things in our lives that aren't ready, that we haven't fully submitted to Him. And let's face it- we like our "busy." We have fallen into the trap of believing that somewhere in our "busy" we will find our purpose and meaning. In reality, "busy" just keeps us too preoccupied to fix our minds on things of eternal value.

What if we turn this whole holiday into what it's meant to be about-Heaven? That was the question that came to me when I was thinking about Advent this year. During the days of study and prayer and research, it became very clear to me that you can't really have a book about our Heavenly home without exploring themes about our earthly homes. It soon became overwhelming, because the Scriptures are packed with references to this theme of "Dwelling." Page after page of notes turned into notebooks, notepads, sticky-notes everywhere. Books started stacking up everywhere with more sticky-notes marking pages. How to narrow this down? It was quite a task, and even now I feel so much has been left out.

But today, after all the very early mornings and very late nights of praying, studying, and writing, you hold in your hands a very simple book about the places where God dwells, and how He longs for us to dwell together with Him. The message preaches itself- what more could my words add to a truth that is so profound?

Clearly, home is important to our Father, and I believe it's also important to us. After all, isn't that truly what Advent reminds us of? We are waiting with increasing anticipation for home. Maybe we don't identify it as such, but those moments when our hearts are taken over by a sense of deep nostalgia and longing for the past- could this also be homesickness? Think about it like this, have you ever wandered through the kitchen to find something to eat, and after opening the refrigerator over and over, and even pillaging through the junk food cabinet, you realize you don't really want anything to eat? Or maybe you find yourself flipping through the channels on television or scrolling the phone or tablet-but nothing catches your eye? You want something, but you just don't know what it is. Maybe in those moments the Holy Spirit is reminding you that this world is not your final home, and because it's not, you will never find full satisfaction here. Ecclesiastes reminds us that eternity is written on our hearts. Sometimes if we listen closely, we can hear it calling to us in those longings that just won't be satisfied.

During Advent, we take the time to consider our lives- how are we living as we wait? Are our hearts prepared to meet the Lord? Have we laid up our treasures in Heaven? Have we spent sufficient time with Him to know His voice?

Maybe during the year you've found you've drifted away from Him. In all the "busy" of life you've just brushed Him off for the sake of the things that are right in front of you. Maybe you've thought, or even spoken, flippantly about Heaven- as if it's ages away. This season of Advent could be your season to come home. Heaven is coming. We needn't think it's not. It will be here in what seems to be the blink of an eye. Our hearts long for it with all of creation. After all, what else are we waiting for?

I hope, as you read these pages and meditate on the Scriptures, you will hear His voice. I pray you will be filled with all manner of goodness as you remember the God Who has made your heart His dwelling place. And I pray your heart overflows with joy and peace to remember the eternal home that's waiting for you.

*I've got a home in Gloryland that outshines the sun.*

# This Year's Mission

*It's been my experience that God speaks to the hearts of His people at the right time and in the right order to accomplish His will in this world. As I was researching and preparing to write this book, I was also praying for the Lord to give me direction for the mission of this book. If you've read my Advent books the past five years you know that each year the proceeds for the annual book sales are always given to missions. This is always a matter of much prayer- the kind of prayer that involves more listening than speaking.*

*This year I'm once again partnering with Grasp International, Inc. David and Christy Grantham have written the following story about Grasp, and I hope you will take the time to read it. The work that David is currently doing with Grasp in Peru, to help rescue and provide homes for children targeted by human traffickers, will amaze you. The money from this year's book will directly support David's work.*

# The Story of Grasp International Inc

In January 2013 a group of likeminded Christian men felt the burden of the many lost souls in southern Peru. As a result of the burden grew a calling to take the gospel there. Grasp International, Inc., **G**od **R**eaching **A**ll of **S**outhern **P**eru, was born. Skip Ferron of Fayetteville, Georgia, established Grasp as a nonprofit and began the process of connecting churches with ministries in Peru with the intent of evangelizing and exposing the people of Peru to the Gospel of Jesus Christ. In 2016, Grasp began teaching seminary classes to indigenous pastors and church leaders in Peru, under the direction of Julio Cruz Arenas and in Kenya Africa, under the direction of Moses Omondi Odhiambo.

In 2019, Grasp began supporting local church planters who graduated from the seminary training. There is a vision to aid, assist, and support the local pastor long enough for the pastor to establish and train his flock. Financial support as well as guidance is given to the pastor for three years and the training will continue for a total of six years.

As a result of immersing ourselves and others in the ministry to the people and pastors of Peru we discovered so many more needs. In 2018, Grasp began building a water filter plant in Tacna, Peru, to provide clean water for Southern Peru. The water plant was completed in 2020 and is managed by Pastor Henry Sucapuca. Nobody could imagine what God had in store, but He was preparing the leaders and board members of Grasp for something BIG.

Grasp isn't only involved in ministry overseas. In 2017, through a generous donation, Grasp acquired 178 acres of beautiful property in Arabi, Georgia, with the intent of emotionally supporting struggling pastors in the states. Shamgar Ministries began partnering with Grasp as Stillwater Pastor Retreat was established. Stillwater has four serene cabins to provide rest for pastors, ministerial staff, missionaries, and para-church ministries. Guests come at no cost to enjoy a large pond, pool, and playground for the kids, but most importantly, they come to rest, unplug, and heal.

July 2022 was a pivotal month for Grasp and we believe what God had been preparing the Grasp ministry leaders for. During a mission trip to Peru under the leadership of David Grantham, President of Grasp, it was discovered that precious children in the Iquitos jungle were being trafficked for sex and organs. The jungles of Peru are a brutal place to raise a child. With no means of education, inferior health conditions, and poor growing conditions, families are often forced to surrender their children. Sex traffickers prey on these vulnerable, naïve, and desperate parents by promising to pay them $3-$5 and to take care of the children, giving them a better life. These parents will never see their children again.

After learning of these atrocities, Grasp has taken a leap of faith and begun the delicate process of legally rescuing these children as well as providing healthcare, Biblical training and discipleship, and private education. The cost for us to legally rescue one child is approximately $2,000 and free to the parents. In addition, parents who wish to stay connected to their children will receive updates and photos.

In January of 2023, Grasp purchased a piece of property in Arequipa, Peru, and began construction on a four-story orphanage for these precious children. The orphanage will provide safe housing for 55-60 children. Because the children coming from the jungle are poorly educated, private tutors must be secured to help with the children's education. God is leading Grasp to establish a school near the orphanage to provide private studies to focus on learning Biblical Discipleship, English, Spanish and other required fields of education. God is so faithful, and He is providing needed funds at every phase of the project.

In all success stories there are always heartaches and trials. Grasp hired a missionary named Gloria in the jungle to watch out for the children and protect them from the traffickers. Once we began legally adopting the children from the jungle, the traffickers realized our strategy and threatened the life of our missionary. She felt compelled to leave the jungle to spare her life. Grasp asks that we all join together in prayer asking our Heavenly Father to bring confusion to the traffickers so that we will not lose any of these precious children.

The Lord has used Grasp International to do so much more than the original leaders could have ever imagined from 2013 until now, and, we trust, into the future.

Visit GraspInternationalInc.com to see pictures of our many ministries in motion. Pastors, ministerial staff, and missionaries can apply for a stay at Stillwater Pastor Retreat through the website as well.

You can contact David Grantham at *DavidGrantham5@yahoo.com* to schedule him to speak to your group, or for information on how you can be involved with the work in Peru, or any of the other places Grasp is working.

Christ by highest Heaven adored
Christ the everlasting Lord
Late in time behold Him come
Offspring of the virgin's womb
Veiled in flesh the Godhead see
Hail the Incarnate Deity
Pleased as man with men to dwell
Jesus our Emmanuel

# Week One

*And God will open wide the gates of heaven for you to enter into the eternal kingdom of our Lord and Savior Jesus Christ.*

— 2 PETER 1:11 (THE LIVING BIBLE)

# December 3, 2023

## WHERE HE DWELLS

There is something about Christmas that turns our thoughts toward home. The season usually begins with our family tradition of bringing out the lights and decorations that we haven't seen in a year. In my house, it's usually an exercise in trying to recall where each particular item belongs, and the older I grow, the more flexible I become with where the decorations will be displayed- namely because I just can't remember where we set it out twelve months ago.

We think of family: Have we covered everyone on our shopping list? Do I have the ingredients for all the cakes, cookies, and candies I will make- and do I have my list to remind me who gets which treats? Arrangements for travel or for family who may be visiting from out of town have to be made. Linens washed, bathrooms scrubbed, furniture polished, food prepared.

But despite the busy-ness of making everything just right for everyone, and despite the stress and anticipation of the inevitable uncomfortable family discussions (every family has them!), underneath it all is a deep knowing that somewhere exists a place called Home, a place I was created to belong.

I recognize that not everyone reading these words has a good experience at home. Not all memories of families are pleasant. There are many people who are living in temporary arrangements, many estranged from family, many who are alone, many who are homeless. No matter what your situation or circumstances may be in this moment, there is a longing that every human being experiences- it is the longing for that place where there is unconditional acceptance and belonging.

Malcolm Muggeridge is considered one of the great journalists and satirists of the 20<sup>th</sup> century; his writings trace not only his experiences and how they changed his political and social viewpoints, but how he traded a life of emptiness as an atheist, for a life of fulfillment and purpose when he became a follower of Jesus. The Lord drew Muggeridge to Himself over a period of time, however, there was one particular moment He used to get the man's attention, and I read about this encounter recently in Os Guiness' book *Signals of Transcendence.*

While serving during World War II in Africa, Muggeridge became over-taken by his sense of isolation and lack of purpose. He felt utterly alone, and felt as if there were nowhere on earth he belonged. These feelings grew over time until one night he was convinced the only solution was to take his own life. He walked down to the ocean and removed his clothes, then swam out into the depths. But as he swam in the cold, dark sea, something caught his eye on shore. From that distance, alone in the darkness, the lights of a little café in the village gripped his heart and created an overwhelming sense of home. This was not a moment of salvation, but it was a redemptive moment nonetheless. For the first time in a long time, Muggeridge felt that he belonged somewhere. Guiness explained that the lights of that little café signaled and called to Muggeridge's heart that, across the wasteland of the earth, there was home, there was the promise of that *something more* he longed for. Somewhere on that shore was where he would find direction, purpose, and destiny.

In Psalm 36, David wrote:

> *How precious is Your*
> *Lovingkindness, O God!*
> *And the children of men take refuge*
> *In the shadow of Your wings.*

*They drink their fill of the*
*Abundance of Your house;*
*And You give them to drink of the*
*River of Your delights.*
*For with You is the fountain of life;*
*In Your light we see light.*

Malcolm Muggeridge, though he didn't know it at that moment, was seeking the abundance that can only be found where the Lord dwells. He was longing for that fountain of life. And God used that little café to start him on his journey to finding the refuge he was truly seeking.

From the moment of man's creation, there was a single place he belonged- that place is with God, His Creator. Reading through the account of creation in Genesis, I find it so comforting that while God spoke everything into existence- the skies, the plants, trees, animals- when it came to man, God used His hands. With deep love and great tenderness, God *formed* man. Then, when it came time to make a home for man, though He could have spoken into existence a beautiful mansion or palace, instead we are told that God *planted* a garden. The home that man was given was fashioned by the hands of God.

When Adam and Eve chose to sin, fellowship between them and God was broken, and it became necessary for them to leave the garden of Eden. Though their address changed temporarily, their destiny and purpose did not. Man was designed and created for fellowship with God- but how could that fellowship happen if they could no longer dwell together? God promised that there would come a time when He would once again dwell with us. That time was Christmas, when Jesus, God's Son, our Emmanuel, came to be born of a virgin. God, once again, got His hands and feet dirty for the sake of mankind as he traveled the country, worked as a carpenter, was nailed to a cross, and buried in a tomb that couldn't hold Him.

We all continue to long for a place called home. We long to return to that garden He planted for us, we long for that eternal dwelling God is now preparing for us. We belong with Him, and as we enter these days of celebration of Christ's birth, our hearts long even more for our

Emmanuel, God With Us. Where He dwells is where we are truly home.

When you think of "Home," what comes to mind? As you prepare your heart for Christmas, think of what it means to you that where God dwells is where we are truly at home.

# December 4, 2023

## GHOST RUNNER

**M**y little town of Perry, GA, is getting a new pizza restaurant. Now look, this is a big deal because I really like pizza. We have the standard chain pizza joints and they're fine. But I was really excited to hear that two local guys, Cody and Wade Walker, are opening a brick and mortar place called Ghost Runner Pizza. For a while now Ghost Runner Pizza has been a pop-up phenomenon, with pizza lovers stalking their social media pages to find out when and where to get some of their amazing pies. Well, at least I've been told it's amazing by friends who speak of it with watering mouths and a happy, far-away look in their eyes. Hopefully I will soon be able to find out for myself.

What an odd name for a pizza place, though, right? Where did such a title come from? If, like me, you have ever played yard ball with the neighborhood kids, you are familiar with the term "ghost runner." Whenever someone had to go home before the game was done- for supper or bath time or a whipping for not doing their chores- their base was then covered by what we called a "ghost runner." This ghost runner, an invisible member of the team, would run the bases and could even score a run- but they could also be tagged out. The key was that everyone had to remember exactly where that ghost runner was supposed to be at each play.

Thinking about those ghost runners got me thinking about how we often have empty bases in our homes and in our lives. But in life those empty places are not simply about a ball game. For those who are setting a table for one, who are making up just one side of the bed, who are packing up a crib that was never filled, these empty bases often create a deep loneliness and sorrow. And no amount of imagination, no ghost runners, can ever fill those places.

In Genesis we read of man's creation. We understand he was created for God's pleasure and for His glory. He was meant to be fulfilled by living in God's presence. And yet God designed and fashioned a second being- the woman. Someone like man, to complement man. In fact, throughout the first two chapters of Genesis, while God was creating and declaring all to be good, this one thing-man's aloneness- was the first thing He declared "not good."

> *"The Lord God said, "It is not good for the man to be alone. I will make a helper suitable for him."*
> Genesis 2:18

God, existing in three persons, being all wise, and governing His creation with kindness and mercy, wanted us to know the same fulfill-ment of living in community with one another that He enjoys as a Triune God who exists in three persons- Father, Son, Holy Spirit. It's very clear that He did not intend for us to be alone. And, contrary to what some people believe, He does intend for us to live in community with one another, that is, with other human beings like us. Though we can be fulfilled solely with His presence during the lonely days of our lives, He created man for community and the enjoyment of dwelling with others.

Our social media-driven culture, however, has idealized being alone over being actually connected to other people. Living in a polarized world has, by all appearances, left many feeling threatened by other people and overly sensitive to criticism and disagreement (both real and perceived). Introversion and social anxiety has become glamourized by the media in general, but is being shown to have detrimental impacts for young and old alike. The ongoing self-isolation ironically being popularized by social media influencers wreaks havoc on the emotional well-being of much of the population. It is leaving empty bases in lives that were meant to be filled, not with ghost runners, but with other people.

We were created for belonging to God and with God, and to others and with others. In this life, we may very well experience those empty places in our earthly homes. But Advent reminds us of Christ Emmanuel, God With Us, and we are comforted to know that He is with us for eternity.

Genesis 1:1 reminds us of the emptiness that existed in the beginning. We read that as His Spirit hovered over that emptiness that He filled the void with light. Again and again in Scripture we see how God's Spirit does that- how He fills those empty places. In Luke 1:35, the angel told Mary,

> *The Holy Spirit will come upon you, and the power of the Most High will overshadow you; and for that reason, the holy Child shall be called the Son of God.*

And in John 14, as Jesus is preparing to leave His disciples for the cross, He promises that He will send His Helper- the Holy Spirit- to dwell in us.

At every point in history since creation itself, God is making it clear that He wants to dwell with us. He wants to fill the empty places in our lives with Himself. It is in His very presence we know and experience fullness of joy (Psalm 16:11). We remember during Advent the quietness of His first coming as a newborn baby, and we fix our hearts on that future moment when He will come with a shout of victory to take us to Heaven where we can enjoy His presence forever.

Are there empty bases in your life today that only God can fill? Pray for a fresh awareness of His Holy Spirit dwelling with you and ask Him to fill you with great joy as you fellowship with Him today.

BE NEAR ME LORD JESUS, I ASK THEE TO STAY
CLOSE BY ME FOREVER, AND LOVE ME, I PRAY.

# December 5, 2023

## HOME FOR CHRISTMAS

It's been said that Bing Crosby's 1943 recording 1943 of the song "I'll Be Home for Christmas" did more to boost the morale of the U.S. military during World War II than any other song or performer. The song was written from the perspective of a soldier serving far from home. All his fondest Christmas memories are listed as his wish for the holiday, even though he realizes being home to experience the snow, the mistletoe, the presents under the tree will just be a dream and not a reality. Ironically, the songwriters initially couldn't find anyone to record the song- everyone felt it was too sad for what should be a joyous season. But Crosby heard the song and disagreed. He was right, and even today the song tugs many heartstrings during the Christmas season.

The longing to be home at Christmas is almost universal. Many books and movies have been written around this theme because it's one that resonates deeply with all of us, no matter how flawed our "home for Christmases" might have been. It's a time when most of us made life-long memories with family and friends, but those memories seem like so much more. These memories are crafted by dearly held traditions, and these traditions provide some feeling of identity and security in who we are. Young parents and new grandparents work hard to recreate those memories and create new traditions for the younger generations- traditions that will continue to draw families together through the years. Most of all, these traditions and relationships with our family connect us to the place we first felt that sense of belonging and value. No wonder our homes are places we want to return to, even if those homes are not ideal.

The sentiment of being home for Christmas, just like Bing Crosby sang, often ends on a somber note. As we age and family and close friends who shared our traditions pass away, or, as is often the case in our modern world, families become fractured through divorce and remarriage, all these things may find us feeling lost during the holidays. But the somber note doesn't need to linger in our hearts, because there's something much better for us to cling to.

In reality, our true sense of belonging and value comes from our identity as a child of God, and the home we deeply long for is Heaven where we will be in the presence of the Lord. The psalmist recognized this longing when he wrote the following in Psalm 27:4-5:

> *One thing I have asked from the Lord, that I shall seek:*
> *That I may dwell in the house of the Lord all the days of my life,*
> *To behold the beauty of the Lord*
> *And to meditate in His temple.*
> *For on the day of trouble He will conceal me in His tabernacle;*
> *He will hide me in the secret place of His tent;*
> *He will lift me up on a rock.*

David, though he was a great warrior and victorious king, knew that the deepest trouble he would ever face was from an enemy that couldn't be defeated with a sword, and that his only protection from that enemy- the enemy of his soul- was in the Lord's tabernacle. During those times when he felt defeated or fearful, David recognized the true longing of his heart was for the presence of God.

One writer has said that all of God's children desire to dwell in their Father's house. Not as a traveler who is just passing through for the night, but to dwell there forever- all the days of our lives, here and now, and for eternity- as children with our Father.

In God's presence is our home, and so, though we can dwell with Him now through the indwelling Holy Spirit, the deeper longing for that physical dwelling place in Heaven is the true longing of our hearts.

In John 14:1-6 we can read the words of comfort that Jesus spoke to His disciples about this:

> *"Do not let your heart be troubled; believe in God, believe also in Me. In My Father's house are many rooms; if that were not so, I would have told you, because I am going there to prepare a place for you. And if I go and prepare a place for you, I am coming again and will take you to Myself, so that where I am, there you also will be. And you know the way where I am going." Thomas said to Him, "Lord, we do not know where You are going; how do we know the way?" Jesus said to him, "I am the way, and the truth, and the life; no one comes to the Father except through Me."*

David Jeremiah wrote that "there's something intimate and sweet and personal about heaven when we talk about it using the same terms our Lord did when He called it "My Father's house." It's no longer an empty space. In our mind's eye, we see a home."

When Jesus was born of Mary all those centuries ago, He was coming to earth to begin the process of taking us home. During Advent, we are to examine our hearts to find those bits of this earthly home we cling to so tightly- so much so that we have forgotten this isn't our final residence. We really do have a Heavenly home waiting for us.

Today, if you're feeling a bit homesick or a bit lost, hide yourself for a while in the Lord's tabernacle so that you can meditate on all He is. As you enjoy the beauty of Christmas in the lights and decorations in your home, let them remind you of the beauty of Christ and of the home He is preparing for you.

LORD, YOU HAVE BEEN OUR DWELLING PLACE IN ALL GENERATIONS.
BEFORE THE MOUNTAINS WERE BORN
OR YOU GAVE BIRTH TO THE EARTH AND THE WORLD,
EVEN FROM EVERLASTING TO EVERLASTING, YOU ARE GOD.
PSALM 90:1-2

# December 6, 2023

## THE GOSPEL COMES WITH A HOUSE KEY

The process of writing this book every year has taken me to a wonderful bed and breakfast in coastal Georgia. It's just a few hours from my house, but it offers a change of scenery and a relief from distractions that vie for my attention at home. Having visited there for several years, the owner-hosts have become friends and it's a joy to spend time with them, but they know I'm there to work. If I take a break and sit in the living room with JoAnn to watch a tennis match on television, she will eventually ask me how my work is coming- a gracious hint and reminder of what I'm really there to do. Many people would say that JoAnn has the gift of hospitality. I believe JoAnn would say she knows the business of hospitality.

The idea that hospitality is a spiritual gift is questionable. It appears in almost every spiritual gifts inventory you might have the opportunity to take, but in reviewing the context of the spiritual gifts passages of Scripture, hospitality seems to be more of a command than a gift. The thing is, God practices hospitality and He has an expectation that we, as beings created in His image, will do the same.

Rosaria Butterfield wrote a book called *The Gospel Comes with a House Key*. Butterfield's salvation was a direct result of the hospitality of a

Christian couple who decided to take the initiative to invite this liberal, feminist, lesbian activist into their home for a meal and conversation. They extended hospitality to her. They taught her the difference between their ability to accept her as a being created in God's image and their inability to approve of her lifestyle- and they assured her that Jesus loved her and they did, too. Today, Rosaria is a follower of Christ and, along with her husband, who is also her pastor, they practice and teach the ministry of hospitality. (If you'd like to read her testimony, she shares it in depth in her book titled *The Secret Thoughts of an Unlikely Convert).*

Almost daily, Rosaria puts on a big pot of soup and bakes bread. Her door is always unlocked and her table is always set. The invitation is always open; some days she may have a dozen people around her table, and other days only her family. Everyone is welcome, but Rosaria and her husband particularly want those who wouldn't necessarily believe they were welcome to know that they have a place.

One of these individuals is a man named Zion. Zion is an inmate in a low-security prison. He is allowed out for five hours every other week and on holidays in order to attend worship. During one visit to the Butterfields Zion told them, "I've never been in a home before...not like this. With love. With Christ. With brothers and sisters. With children. And I belong, too. Here." Butterfield writes, "The Gospel comes with a house key. When table fellowship includes those from prison, orphan-hood, and poverty in real and abiding ways, permanent bonds of care and kinship are the consequences."

Later she writes the following:

> "Hospitality is the obvious bridge that brings desperate people into a Christian home, where they can both receive and give great blessings. But the question is: Do Christian people prac-tice Christian hospitality in regular, ordinary, consistent ways? Or do we think our home too precious for criminals and outcasts? Our homes are not our castles. Indeed, they are not even ours."

Inviting others into our homes for fellowship creates in us a deeper understanding of what it means to live under the hospitality of God as our dwelling place. We remember being unwanted and unworthy, and now we are welcomed guests. We remember the lifechanging moment we went from hopeless to hopeful, from unloved to greatly loved, from empty to filled up, from broken to mended. We were accepted by God as we were, and as He allowed us to dwell together with Him, He began, and continues, to transform us through the redemptive work of Jesus and the sanctifying work of His Holy Spirit.

Think about it this way: If, as Scripture assures us, God is, and always has been, our dwelling place- imagine all such a thing means for us. I know I'm not always the best house guest. I try not to break someone's best china, but I'm not going to promise I won't drop a few crumbs of cornbread on the floor. When it comes to dwelling in the presence of God, my spiritually messy life will require deep grace on the part of my Host. When we, in obedience, seek to be that gracious host for others with their spiritually messy lives, what a transformative work we are able to witness.

As I meditate on this command to hospitality, especially in this season of Advent, I'm reminded of the Christ-child, whose first bed was a manger, surrounded by the lowly, unclean shepherds fresh out of the fields- shepherds who had been specifically invited by the angels to come to Bethlehem to see the Bread of Life. I'm also reminded of that glorious day when we will be sitting around a grander table at the marriage supper of the Lamb.

And I wonder if there will be anyone around that table who met Christ around mine.

Today reach out to the Lord with gratitude that He has extended to us an invitation to dwell with Him for all eternity. Ask Him to give you the opportunities and the grace to practice the hospitality that He has exhibited to you.

# December 7, 2023

## HOMEMAKING

Over the past few months of researching for this book, I have developed a new habit. Let me explain... Apparently, when you start searching topics on various search engines, the robot inside your computer decides to get involved. Pretty soon, every website you visit offers suggestions about what you've been searching. Google is my default search engine. YouTube is my go-to for music, Bible studies, and some of my favorite preaching. Apparently, Google and YouTube are BFFs, so when I started asking Google to show me information on "home," Google told YouTube and YouTube said, "Hold my cocoa! I got you!" Turns out, there are hundreds of YouTube channels devoted to the topic of homemaking. I've found a couple (well, five) channels that I really enjoy and can find myself getting caught up in new ideas- things like how to clean a showerhead or ways to style my Christmas vignettes. "Vignettes" is a fancy way of referring to the empty places around your house that you creatively arrange all the decorations you bring home from Hobby Lobby.

Let me repeat myself, in case you forgot it in your excitement about that showerhead and all the vignettes you plan on setting up this year- there are **hundreds** of channels devoted to homemaking. Currently, 335 channels. At first, this amazed me. But after watching for a while it occurred to me that many of the people who are watching and subscribing to these channels belong to a generation of homemakers who, most likely, never had to make their own beds or clean a showerhead. While home-bound during the pandemic, many people realized the enormity of keeping a house and making a home and realized how poorly equipped they were to do so. Where do you go these days to learn how to do anything? YouTube, of course. Learning how to clean, declutter, meal plan, and a dozen ways to make a simple biscuit, gives a sense of satisfaction and fulfillment to homemaking and more people have begun to truly enjoy their homes.

King David's son, Solomon, didn't have YouTube with over 300 channels to reference when he built the Temple in Jerusalem. Solomon was commissioned by God to build the Temple, the sanctuary for the Lord. 2 Chronicles 28 tells us that the plans for the Temple were given to him by his father, David, who had received them from God. It took Solomon seven years to build the Temple to the very detailed specifications that God had given David. We are given quite a breathtaking description of what happened when the work on the Temple was complete and the priests and other attendants entered for the first time:

> ...and when they raised their voices accompanied by trumpets, cymbals, and other musical instruments, and when they praised the Lord saying, "He indeed is good for His kindness is everlasting," then the house, the house of the Lord, was filled with a cloud, so that the priests could not rise to minister because of the cloud, for the glory of the Lord filled the house of God.
> (2 Chronicles 5:13-14)

What a humbling moment this must have been for Solomon and for all of God's people. A house had been built for God's glory to dwell with them. And God's glory filled the Temple. His presence was here on Earth with His people- the ones He loved and the ones He has always longed to dwell with.

Gradually, though, the lure of disobedience began to tug on the hearts of God's people. Again and again they went astray. Oh, they would come back, but it was harder to find those who were single-mindedly devoted to God alone. Their devotion was temporary, and almost always divided.

God has always wanted us to be completely His for all eternity. And so, what man could not accomplish- an eternal Temple where we can dwell together with Him- God stepped in to accomplish. He sent Jesus.

In Ephesians 2, Paul tells us that we, the church, *"are being fitted together...(and)...growing into a holy temple in the Lord, in whom you also are being built together into a dwelling of God in the Spirit."* Later, Peter tells us we are living stones who are being built up into a spiritual house.

This all may seem a little technical and detailed and maybe a little bit heavy, but the truth of what is happening here- of what is happening in you and in me- is absolutely beautiful.

God is in Heaven, and we are on earth until He calls us home or returns for us. God desires a place He can dwell with us, and our desire is to be restored to Him, but He also sees our utter helplessness to accomplish that restoration on our own. So, He came down from Heaven and did an inscrutable spiritual work. Through His perfect redemption, He flawlessly draws us to Him and makes us- you and me- His dwelling place.

Because of His Holy Spirit dwelling in us, we now have the power to overcome the lure of disobedience that tugs us away from Him. We sit in a position of being justified with all our sins atoned for. And we wait for the day He will come again to take us to our Heavenly home where we will dwell with Him face-to-face for all eternity. None of this is because of anything we have done. It's all because of Him and His great love for us.

One of the blessings of Advent is that it pulls our attention away from all the busyness of the season and back onto the One Christmas is all about. It reminds us to take the time to remember that God wanted to dwell with us so much that He broke through the barriers of space and time just to come and make a way for that to happen. On those days we may feel He is far away from us, we can remember that one day He will return to take us to Heaven to dwell with Him forever.

Take the time today to thank God for making His home in your heart. Let Him fill your heart with deep joy in knowing that He will dwell with you for all eternity.

# December 8, 2023

Linda Smith Davis has created an entire business devoted specifically to fine living. She is the creator and owner of a business called New England Fine Living, with a large following on social media and her website. She takes her viewers and readers along on her journey of renovating and decorating her historic New England homes, including landscaping and gardening. Her videos show her doing much of the work herself, and I've been particularly inspired by her adept use of a nail gun and jig saw. It's this hard work ethic Linda depicts that draws us in- not just the hard work, but the obvious satisfaction she gets from it, even when her projects don't turn out exactly as planned. Her motto, or mission statement perhaps, is that we all can discover our own version of fine living, "no matter how simple or grand that might be." In other words, we don't have to spend a lot of money or take on projects beyond our abilities to experience fine living. We just have to learn that there is joy and fulfillment in using what we have to make our homes the best they can be.

In Isaiah 54, God told the Israelites who were in exile to:

> *Enlarge the place of your tent;*
> *Stretch out the curtains of your dwellings, spare not.*
> *Lengthen your cords and strengthen your pegs.*

The Israelites were in Babylon. They had lost everything and were living under the judgment of God because of their idolatry. Now God was telling them to prepare for restoration, and not just being restored to their previous condition, but so much better- restored and improved. How could this be?

Continuing in this chapter is a beautiful promise and love letter from their Father:

> *"For a brief moment I forsook you,*
> *But with great compassion I will gather you.*
> *In an outburst of anger I hid my face from you for a moment,*
> *But with everlasting lovingkindness I will have compassion on you,"*
> *Says the Lord your Redeemer. (verses 7-8)*
> *For the mountains may be removed and the hills may shake,*
> *But My lovingkindness will not be removed from you,*
> *And my covenant of peace will not be shaken,"*
> *Says the Lord who has compassion on you.*
> *"O afflicted one, storm-tossed, and not comforted,*
> *Behold, I will set your stones in antimony,*
> *And your foundations I will lay in sapphires.*
> *Moreover, I will make your battlements of rubies,*
> *And your gates of crystal,*
> *And your entire wall of precious stones.*
> *All your sons will be taught of the Lord;*
> *And the well-being of your sons will be great.*
> *In righteousness you will be established..." (verses 10-14)*

So many times throughout this passage we read the words *compassion* and *lovingkindness*. Our hearts are in wonder at the beauty of the city that God is preparing to be our home with the sapphires, rubies, crystals, and precious stones. For the Israelites this prophecy held the promise of the Messiah who would come to teach their sons and establish His people in righteousness. But there's also the promise of an eternal home in Heaven, where we will be free from oppression and from fear, because at the time of Christ's second Advent all of His enemies will be destroyed.

I'm reminded today that through God's grace and generous provision and through the exercise of good stewardship of His gifts, I can live a beautiful life here and now. Because His Holy Spirit dwells with me, I can enjoy everything He offers to me as my Heavenly Father. But this earthly home, no matter how wonderful it is, can never compare to the home He is preparing.

The manger, the cross, the tomb- places that were so pivotal during Jesus' first advent- those physical places have faded away with time. But the power of what occurred there changed the course of human life- because what happened in those places secured our eternal home in Heaven.

Our earthly home will fade away, the décor will wear out, the walls will need repainting, the lights will dim. Along with its joys, this home will also experience sorrow and sickness and loss. Not so with the home that will be mine the next time Jesus comes. That home, with its foundations in the righteousness of my Savior, will be eternally beautiful and serene, filled with glory and light.

Take the time today to thank God for the home He has given you here on earth. Thank Him that His Word promises a better home that is yet to come, and praise Him that because we know He is always true to His promises, we can look forward with great hope to dwelling with Him in Heaven when He returns for us.

# December 9, 2023

## POSSUM TROT, TEXAS

I n 1996 Donna's Martin's mother died. Donna was one of twenty-one children born to her mother, Martha Lee Grisby. Donna describes the depression she felt after losing her mother, a depression so deep that she asked God to either heal her or let her die. God answered by placing a very special call on her life. In the quiet of her kitchen, the Lord reminded her that there are thousands of children who would never know the relationship she had had with her mother-or any parent at all. And there, over a sink filled with dirty dishes, the Lord called Donna to the ministry of foster care and adoption.

She shared this revelation with her husband, W.C. Martin, who was the pastor of Bennett Chapel Missionary Baptist Church, and he then shared it with their congregation. By 1997 the first child was adopted in Possum Trot out of foster care. By 2005, twenty-three families in this rural unincorporated town in east Texas, with a population of about 700 people, had adopted 72 children.

Working together as a congregation, a community, and with state agencies, the people of Possum Trot (who are mostly working class African-American families with an average income of $40,000 per year) were able to figure out the *how* of this ministry. The *why* had already been figured out for them.

W.C. Martin told World Magazine's *Effective Compassion Podcast*, "Adoption is not a man-made thing. It started with God. God purposely started adoption...(because)... the only way for a man to get back to God was through adoption through Jesus Christ." Martin is referring here to Paul's teaching in Romans 8:15 that we have not received the spiritual standing of a slave, but instead we've received the spiritual standing of an adopted child with all the legally binding and relational privileges with God our Father.

Scriptures clearly show that God's people are not to be just recipients of this adoption, but to show God's love by taking care of orphans and widows. Thirteen years ago when pastoring in the metro-Birmingham, AL, area, David Platt preached a message from James 1:27, which defines pure religion as the practice of "visiting orphans and widows in their distress." The next week after delivering that sermon, Platt reached out to the Department of Human Resources, the agency that handled foster care and adoptions for their county. During that conversation he discovered about 150 families were needed to place the children currently in foster care. Platt's church hosted a meeting with the Alabama Children's Home and the state child welfare agency- over 800 families attended, and over 150 of those families signed up to assist with the needs of the children in foster care. That was the beginning of the foster and adoption ministry of that church, which is still active and flourishing today.

Back in Texas, Donna tells the story of Mercedes, a little girl they adopted when she was five. The little girl had been taught by her birth mother to steal food. It took years for them to break that habit of stealing. Donna tells of asking the Lord, "What do I do about this situation?" In answer to that prayer, the Lord showed her that she needed to put herself in that child's shoes. "I had to become that child," Donna explained.

With that statement, she summed up the story, the *how* and the *why*, of Christmas. How else would God bring us home to where He dwells but through adoption through His Son? How else would Christ provide for our perfect redemption and count us as righteous but through becoming like us, coming in the form of a man? And why? Because like the least of these orphaned children we could never have done it on our own. We never could have provided for our own salvation, nor would we have ever even known such salvation was possible. But God came down to us, so that we could be brought up to Him.

Today, thank God for your standing as His heir. Thank Him for sending Jesus to accomplish what we could never have done for ourselves. Praise Him for the work of salvation that was begun in Bethlehem.

During these days of Advent consider ways that you can be a part of helping in this area of foster care and adoption. How can you support foster parents and those seeking adoption in your church or community?

(Take a moment to look up CarePortal and the Global Orphan Project online, which offer ways that churches and individuals can help meet the needs of those in foster care.)

For lo, the days are hastening on,
By prophets seen of old
When with the ever circling years
Shall come the time foretold

# Week Two

*The people who walk in darkness*
*Will see a great light;*
*Those who live in a dark land*
*The light will shine upon them*
*Isaiah 9:2*

# $\mathscr{D}ecember\ 10,\ 2023$

## THE LIST

The Department of Christmas Affairs (DCA) is a fictional North Pole Government agency that supports Santa's work by maintaining The List. You know the one. The Naughty/Nice List. Though the legend of Santa Clause can be traced as far back as the 3rd century, there was never a mention of a list until the early 1930's when the song "Santa Clause is Coming to Town" was popularized.

According to their website, www.christmasaffairs.com, the DCA uses the "Global Behaviour Tracking network and data-mining technology to determine who will be in good favour come Christmas." I am happy to say that my name has been on the Nice section of The List for the past year. (I checked both the formal and the familiar versions of my name, just to be on the safe side.) However, should I slip up and find myself on the other side of things, the DCA allows me the opportunity to contest that ruling. They also offer rehabilitation with coaches who will, among other things, help you to find the perfect naughty/nice balance.

Santa's List is a fun tradition that brings back lots of memories of Christmases past. Occasionally you may encounter someone who was traumatized and scarred for life because of it, and that's sad to me because as a child everything Santa-related brought a feeling of mystery and expectation to Christmas, a sense that the world was a little bit better and lots more fun for a while. And honestly, the idea that somewhere was a list marking how I was doing in life gave me the mindset of checking my behavior and my attitude. So, in a sense, the thought of Santa's List did for me in my (very Southern Baptist) childhood what the season of Advent has done for me as an adult. It gave me the mindset of preparing for the arrival of Jesus- because even though Santa visited our home at Christmas, it was understood that Santa was celebrating the birth of Christ with us.

Recently I was listening to a sermon about Heaven by Louie Giglio, pastor of Passion Church in Atlanta, Georgia. He made the following statement- "If you are a believer, you are a citizen of Heaven. So start living like it." Now, the thing about living like a citizen of Heaven is not that we should try to be good enough, but it's that we continue about our lives knowing that this world is not really where we belong. I love the passage in Colossians 3:1-4:

*"Therefore if you have been raised up with Christ, keep seeking the things above, where Christ is, seated at the right hand of God. Set your mind on the things above, not on the things that are on earth. For you have died and your life is hidden with Christ in God. When Christ, who is our life, is revealed, then you also will be revealed with Him in glory."*

In this passage, Paul goes on to remind us that when we keep our minds fixed on Heaven- our home- it will completely change how we approach our lives. Not because of any ability to fix our poor, sinful behavior on our own, but because changing our mindset is a complete yielding of our lives to Jesus, and obedience is the result of that yielding.

Now, changing our mindset should definitely change our behavior. But in I Thessalonians 5, Paul writes that it's God who will sanctify us entirely. In verse 24 he reminds us that it is our Lord Jesus Christ who will make us complete and without blame. This gives me great hope. You see, there are some things in my life that I just don't seem able to fix. One of the biggest battles I face, that I think is rather common, is the battle with my attitude. I have prayed, confessed, and yielded- time and again- and yet I still keep feeling defeated. As much as I have struggled, I have seen that I just don't have the ability in my flesh to conquer this battle. At times when I am sitting there in defeat once again, I am reminded of the simple power of Christmas, summed up in one little sentence- *"...you shall call His name Jesus, for He will save His people from their sins."*

He will save me from my sins. He will. Stop and think about that for a moment. It's in His very name- *Jesus*- the name that means Savior. His birth, life, death, and resurrection all provided the sacrificial covering we would need for the atonement of our sins- for all of our sins, even the ones we feel powerless against. The writer of Hebrews tells us that because of Jesus we have been released from the fearfulness of Mount Sinai- that place where the Law was given, a law that none of us could keep perfectly. Now we have been granted entry to Mount Zion, the city of the living God. Obviously this doesn't mean that I can live any way I please- no, those of us who are citizens of Heaven will recognize we have a responsibility to live like it.

Now about that list... Isaiah 4:3 tells us that, *"It will come about that he who is left in Zion and remains in Jerusalem will be called holy- everyone who is recorded for life in Jerusalem."* When we come to Christ in faith, our citizenship changes and our names are recorded *for life*. The connotation is that "for life" means as long as I exist- which will be for eternity. My name is not just recorded as a citizen of Zion (the city of God, or Heaven) but I'm recorded as *holy*. I often wonder how that can be. On even my best days, I feel far from holy. Even on a good day I'm an easy target for temptation. But I read that verse again and see that I *will be called holy*. How? Because I have been raised with Christ. Hebrews 12:23 tells me that I belong among those who *are enrolled in Heaven*.

Yes, there really is a list. But that list is not about those who've been good and those who've been bad- it's about who belongs to our Heavenly Father. Psalm 87 is an amazing chapter of Scripture. It pictures the Lord registering His people in Zion. The psalmist names Rahab (Egypt), Babylon, Philistia, and Tyre- these are His enemies! But, as the Lord counts them He states, "This one was born here."

His enemies? Not anymore! How? Why? Because this salvation, this place on His list, is offered to all who will believe. He will save us from our sins.

Today, take some time to be still with the thought that He will save you. Yield those places where you struggle to Him, and thank Him that He will save you. Once you belong to Him, He will no longer consider you His enemy, but His child. What would your life look like, how would your days go differently, if you kept your mind truly fixed on the things above, in Heaven, and not on things of the earth? After all, that's exactly where you belong.

## PSALM 87: THE PRIVILEGES OF CITIZENSHIP IN ZION

*His foundation is in the holy mountains.*
*The Lord loves the gates of Zion*
*More than all the other dwelling places of Jacob.*
*Glorious things are spoken of you,*
*O city of God. Selah.*
*"I shall mention Rahab and Babylon among those who know me;*
*Behold, Philistia and Tyre with Ethiopia:*
*'This one was born there.'"*
*But of Zion it shall be said, "This one and that one were born in*
*her."*
*And the Most High Himself will establish her.*
*The Lord will count when He registers the peoples.*
*"This one was born there." Selah*
*Then those who sing as well as those who play the flutes shall say,*
*"All my springs of joy are in you."*

# December 11, 2023

## FINDING MY PLACE

Ches McCartney ran away from his home in Iowa when he was 14 years old. People who knew him during his childhood described him as odd- he never seemed to fit in with everyone else. From 1930 to 1987, people would see Ches riding up and down the Eastern United States in a wagon pulled by a team of at least nine goats. He was known as the Goat Man, and he made his way by preaching sermons for love offerings, and selling postcards of himself with his goat-pulled rig. His fans could purchase these postcards for 25 cents each or three for a dollar. My co-worker Jimmy is the proud owner of one of those cards. He remembers the Goat Man setting up camp not far from his childhood home in Lizella, Georgia. All the neighbors would gather around to chat with McCartney. When it began to get dark, his parents would make him go home. He said he couldn't understand why anyone would ever want to cut a gathering like that short!

Ches and his son eventually settled in middle Georgia, where his son Albert Gene lived on some property in Twiggs County, while Ches lived out his final years in a nursing home in Macon. He died there in 1998, not long after his son was murdered on their property. Georgia seems a long way from Iowa, so some may say that the Goat Man was far from home. But for Ches McCartney, his home was with his goats and his son, living the life of adventure he had crafted for himself on the roads he loved to travel.

Some people spend their entire lives searching for the place they belong. This need to belong to a place and a group is intrinsic- it's how our Creator designed us. Living in this modern mobile society creates a set of challenges for those who find it difficult to feel connected. Now we battle the saturation of our world and our lives with social media platforms where the more connected we are online the more disconnected we are in real life. For many people, this sense of disconnectedness is a problem.

In Acts 17 the Apostle Paul tells us that our appointed times and the specific geographical location where we live is part of God's eternal plan. The time and the places we live have been ordained by God so we will seek Him and find Him. In verse 28 Paul writes, *"for in Him we live and move and exist."* If we never seek God, if we continue to believe that our lives and our places in this world are all about ourselves, we will miss out on finding reason for our existence and our lives will feel meaningless.

It's fascinating to think the place we live is important to God. The neighbors He has placed around us are there so that we can interact with them and be involved in helping them find the God they are seeking. The same is true with people at our church and people at our jobs. All the interactions we have every day may seem random, but they are very carefully orchestrated by a God Who wants everyone to know Him. God never gets your address wrong. He is in the business of putting all of us right where He wants us to be for His purposes. While we are struggling and striving to always look for that next great home, a step-up to a more affluent subdivision, or a down-sizing to an easier lifestyle, maybe we should be reminded of how important it is to stay where we are long enough to build Gospel-centered God honoring relationships and wait for Him to move us when and where He wants.

His timing is always perfect- we know this, but how often do we patiently submit to it? Galatians 4 tells us that Jesus's birth happened *"when the fullness of the time came."* That means that all the cultural, political, and religious conditions were all lined up in just the right way to carry out His plan to redeem mankind.

What's the answer then for those who feel like they don't belong, who are always seeking to find where they feel accepted as part of a place and a group of people? Perhaps it's a matter of God stirring us to relocate. In many cases that drive to seek a place of acceptance is truly the Lord tugging at us to seek Him- whether for the first time, or just to grow closer to Him.

But it's also possible the feeling we have of not belonging is our signal from God to break out of our comfort zones and engage with the people right here, right now. The Advent season is such a natural time to practice hospitality by opening your home to your neighbors, or even knocking on their doors to deliver gifts and greetings. Perhaps there is someone right next door just waiting for you to share with them the good news of Christmas.

Take a moment and think about this moment in history you've been given. What are the issues we're facing in our world? Maybe it's tempting to look away from the violence, the racial tensions, the poverty, the sexual confusion and perversion and just focus on the parts of these days we feel comfortable with. But there's a reason God has you here now, in this world, in this time in history- and that reason is not to bury your head in the sand or to stand in judgment. The reason we're here is to partner with the Lord's redemptive work in our world in these final days before He returns.

It's terribly important for us to remember that our current address is not our final address. All of us will carry a nagging sense of the need for something more- of being out of place- until we step into Heaven and are finally face-to-face with Jesus. But while we wait, let's give thanks for our homes, and pray for opportunities to connect with the people God has placed next door, across the street, or one cubicle over.

Pray for the people around you today. Ask the Lord to show you needs they may have or ways you can offer encouragement to them. Ask God for the grace and the courage to step out of your comfort zone and connect with someone today who needs to know how much God loves them.

So Joseph also went up from the town of Nazareth in
Galilee to Judea, to Bethlehem the town of David,
because he belonged to the house and line of David.
Luke 2:4

# December 12, 2023

Beautifully decorated Christmas trees stand in front of the two living room windows. The lights are dark, but the ornaments glitter in the natural light of the room. Decorations are scattered around, some still in boxes- waiting to be placed, waiting to adorn the home for the Christmas season. But the home is littered with trash, broken glass, and discarded clothes and other items. The home was abandoned, and Carter Banks, known as BigBankz on YouTube, is documenting it all on video.

Carter is an urban explorer. His channel has over 400,000 subscribers, and his videos have received nearly 50 million views. Like hundreds of other "urb-exers," he finds abandoned homes and other structures, and films what's inside. Many times he finds homes in the same condition as the home described above- homes that look as if the residents just walked away in the middle of their normal routine, and never returned. In these homes he finds family photos, clothes, important letters and other documents, and sometimes items that are likely heirlooms. Then, when he makes his way through the kitchen in these locations, like every young man who has ever lived, he always opens the refrigerator, and almost always immediately regrets it!

All the things he finds, though once so important to the people who lived in these homes, have now been neglected for decades and are in various states of decay. Carter is careful to protect the location of the sites he films, and he treats everything with respect and regard for how fragile they are. He tells me he started exploring out of curiosity about these buildings which are potentially filled with forgotten memories. He believes, and the numbers of viewers of his videos would attest, this is a curiosity shared by millions of people, but most of us are not able to get inside these places to see them for ourselves.

Watching Carter's videos, it's natural to wonder about my own life and home. I'm reminded that all our beautiful homes and all our possessions are just things. Though they may be tangible proofs of a life once lived, they are not our lives. A home filled with possessions is just a big box of stuff when there's no life inside of it.

When the Christ child was born on Christmas all those years ago, He brought with Him life eternal to all of mankind, all who would accept Him by faith. The fall of Adam and Eve in the Garden of Eden, brought loss and despair into the world- far from the place of fullness and abundance God intended to share with His children.

Sin and the enemy of our souls, Satan, has completely distorted our understanding of what fullness and abundance in life means. Our flesh, bound to this world, can only understand abundance in terms of what we can see, so we tend to think our dissatisfaction and discontentment with life can be satisfied with more possessions- bigger and better houses, cars, physical health, a bigger bank account, more prestigious relationships.

Many people work hard all their lives trying to position themselves for *more* in the belief that their peace and abundance can only be acquired through affluence. Millions today are like those the Lord speaks of in Isaiah 65:11, who *"set a table for Fortune and fill cups with mixed wine for Destiny."* These are people who worship the gods of the world in their pursuit of earthly wealth and contentment, but God tells us this will ultimately lead to their ruin and destruction. We see this around us every day because we see the stress, anxiety, and fear that comes with the pursuit of more of what the world has to offer.

The hunger and thirst that we have for satisfaction is not in itself a bad thing. It's a hunger God has given us, meant to lead us to the only source of our satisfaction- Himself. In John 10:10 Jesus said it this way,

*"I came that they may have life, and have it abundantly."*

In this verse we see that the resolution and fulfillment of all our desires is in Him and what He offers us. The truth is, this world can never offer us what He can. All the world offers is bound for decay and destruction. Instead, God tells us,

*"For behold, I create a new heavens and a new earth.*
*And the former things will not be remembered or come to mind.*
*But be glad and rejoice forever in what I create;*
*For behold, I create Jerusalem for rejoicing*
*And her people for gladness.*
*I will also rejoice in Jerusalem*
*And be glad in My people;*
*And there will no longer be heard in her*
*The voice of weeping and the sound of crying."*
*Isaiah 65:17-19*

This gladness and rejoicing is found in Him alone, in His presence in our lives. Notice in these verses that we are meant to share this joy and gladness together with God- mutually enjoying one another- our Father with His children- for all eternity.

And so we remember that our God came to earth to fill us with Himself- Who, as Jesus' mother, Mary, declared, "has filled the hungry with good things." He became like us in order to once and for all accomplish our redemption and to give us the assurance of the inheritance He has secured for us in Heaven, an inheritance that will never perish, spoil, or fade (1 Peter 1:4).

Take some time to read the poem, "Only One Life," by C.T. Studd on the next page. As a missionary, Studd sought to pursue those things in his life that would last for eternity. This familiar poem is a reminder to be mindful of how we order the days of our lives.

Today, let the truth of John 10:10 bring peace to your mind and your heart. Take the time to express your gratitude to Jesus for coming to earth to bring you abundant life, and for the promise of the inheritance that His work of redemption secured for you. Realize that because Christ dwells in you as the hope of glory (Colossians 1:27), the gladness and rejoicing God has promised can begin right here and right now. May this reminder fill you with joy this Christmas.

## ONLY ONE LIFE: C.T. STUDD

*Two little lines I heard one day, Traveling along life's busy way;*
*Bringing conviction to my heart, And from my mind would not depart;*
*Only one life, 'twill soon be past, Only what's done for Christ will last.*
*Only one life, yes only one, Soon will its fleeting hours be done;*
*Then, in 'that day' my Lord to meet, And stand before His Judgment seat;*
*Only one life, 'twill soon be past, Only what's done for Christ will last.*
*Only one life, the still small voice, Gently pleads for a better choice*
*Bidding me selfish aims to leave, And to God's holy will to cleave;*
*Only one life, 'twill soon be past, Only what's done for Christ will last.*
*Only one life, a few brief years, Each with its burdens, hopes, and fears;*
*Each with its days I must fulfill, living for self or in His will;*
*Only one life, 'twill soon be past, Only what's done for Christ will last.*
*When this bright world would tempt me sore, When Satan would a*
*victory score;*
*When self would seek to have its way, Then help me Lord with joy to say;*
*Only one life, 'twill soon be past, Only what's done for Christ will last.*
*Give me Father, a purpose deep, In joy or sorrow Thy word to keep;*
*Faithful and true what e'er the strife, Pleasing Thee in my daily life;*
*Only one life, 'twill soon be past, Only what's done for Christ will last.*
*Oh let my love with fervor burn, And from the world now let me turn;*
*Living for Thee, and Thee alone, Bringing Thee pleasure on Thy throne;*
*Only one life, "twill soon be past, Only what's done for Christ will last.*
*Only one life, yes only one, Now let me say, "Thy will be done";*
*And when at last I'll hear the call, I know I'll say 'twas worth it all";*
*Only one life, 'twill soon be past, Only what's done for Christ will last.*

# December 13, 2023

INVASIVE

In the Springtime, it begins. The small, delicate purple flowers appear along the fence line in the backyard. Glistening with dew in the morning light, they add a welcome bit of color to chase away the gray of winter. By early summer, they have taken over everything I'm trying to grow, and I find myself, armed with a shovel, grunting-sweating-cussing, as I try to dig up every last root of those evil wicked plants, now growing profusely in enormous tight clumps. It is the dreaded Spiderwort, and I've recently learned that people will actually purchase these from seed catalogs or nurseries. One Etsy vendor is currently selling them at a price of three for $18.95. Listen, if you're inclined to grow these, I'll be happy to share some of mine. Free to a good home.

In researching how to eliminate invasive plants like Spiderwort, I've discovered the answer is fairly simple- dig them up by the roots, then immediately plant something in the empty space large enough to absorb the nutrients and sunlight that the Spiderwort is using to self-propagate. This makes sense, because our problem began when we had to remove a row of mature, but diseased, Red Tip trees planted along the other side of the fence. Those trees had kept the fence line shaded enough that the sun-loving evil wicked Spiderwort couldn't grow. Now I am tending new trees that have replaced the Red Tips, and also planting other shrubs along the fence- but in the meantime, the Spiderwort is refusing to let go. I have my work cut out for me.

This has been a good lesson to me, not just in horticulture, but also life in general. It's really easy to passively allow invasive habits and thoughts to take over, things that appear pretty and pleasurable at first but soon block the light, keeping things that are truly good from growing. Seeds of darkness and destruction can be planted in our hearts in so many ways. Our media-driven culture is all about selling us things that we don't really need, and they do that by getting our attention with things that seem good and harmless, and in some cases even truly necessary.

Whether we realize it or not, our language and conversations are influenced by marketing strategies, including social media "influencers," that target the particular demographics we fit into. Surely our infinite God foresaw this when He instructed His people (us) to write His words on the doorposts of our home in Deuteronomy 6:9- not in a literal sense, but meaning that our homes should, from the moment we step through the door, be a place where God's Word is our shield from the wickedness in the outside world that seeks to destroy our families and our homes.

When we dwell in the shelter of the Most High and abide in the shadow of the Almighty (Psalm 91:1), we are protected from those awful invasive and destructive habits and thoughts. Goodness and righteousness and fullness will grow in our lives as we absorb the light that comes from Him alone, starving those things that will destroy us spiritually. Psalm 92 describes the life of righteousness like this:

> *The righteous man will flourish like the palm tree,*
> *He will grow like a cedar in Lebanon.*
> *Planted in the house of the Lord,*
> *They will flourish in the courts of our God.*
> *They will still yield fruit in old age;*
> *They shall be full of sap and very green,*
> *To declare that the Lord is upright;*
> *He is my rock, and there is no unrighteousness in Him.*

That's a great promise! But how do we get there? How do we claim this promise for our own lives? Jeremiah 17:7 tells us that it's simply by faith in God- by confessing that He is our only hope. If our faith is truly in God, then we will live according to the light of His truth. In His Messiah promise in Isaiah 9:2, God tells us *the people who walk in darkness will see a great light; those who live in a dark land, the light will shine on them."* In Zacharias's prophecy about his son John (Luke 1:79), we learn that light will come when the Messiah finally arrives.

One of the best ways we can live in the light of His truth is to follow Paul's direction in Colossians 3:1-2 to keep our minds on Heaven. In fact, every believer should be thinking aggressively about Heaven in our everyday life. If our hearts and lives are so crowded with Heaven, there will be no space for wickedness to invade. Paul writes, *"...keep seeking the things above, where Christ is, seated at the right hand of God. Set your mind on the things above, not on the things that are on earth."*

Maybe today you recognize you've been battling with invasive thoughts or habits in your life that are keeping you from flourishing, making you feel dry and withered in your spirit instead of "full of sap and very green." Ask the Lord to show you those things that need to be uprooted. He will give you the grace to do that. Confess your faith and trust in Him every day and find peace in knowing that by faith you have the privilege of dwelling with Him, planted in the house of the Lord.

# December 14, 2023

## FOLLOWING A STAR HOME

The Wise Men are key figures in the Christmas story, but biblically they are somewhat of a mystery. Though we can kind of piece together some clues about who they were or where they came from, there isn't a key passage of Scripture that give us a lot of detail about them. Maybe it's the mystery that makes us want to know more about them. Considering the fact that we don't know much about who they were, perhaps the important thing is to focus on what they did.

First, they saw the star in the East, which, we presume, is the general area in relation to Bethlehem, where they lived. Now, if you take a look at Matthew 2:2 in your Bible, there's a cross reference by that phrase "His star." A cross reference is a little like a road map, that shows you other places in Scripture you might find the same phrase or idea. The cross reference for "His star" is Numbers 24:17:

*I see him, but not now;*
*I behold him, but not near;*
*A star shall come forth from Jacob,*
*A scepter shall rise from Israel...*

These words are part of a prophecy spoken by a man named Balaam to the king of Midian- one of Israel's enemies- during the time the Israelites were wandering in the wilderness. Balaam was from a cult of prophets who practiced magic and divination. Eventually he was identified as a false prophet who ultimately led Israel away from God, but in this case, Scripture tells us that the spirit of God came over him and he spoke the words that God gave him. These words prophesied the coming Messiah, the Christ. Interestingly, the wise men in Matthew, called Magi, were also magicians and practiced astrology (the practice of predicting the future using the stars). This tells me that our merciful God reaches out to us where we are, even in our messes, to let us know He is here with us. Doesn't this make such perfect sense? He doesn't wait for us to come within the sound of church bells- He comes after us in the dark and ugly places.

The second thing the wise men did was to follow the leading of the star that God showed them. They simply came to where Christ was. Since we don't know exactly where they were from, it's hard to pinpoint how far they traveled or how long it took them. We do know that traveling for long distances in those days was not as easy as packing some snacks in the SUV and hopping on the Interstate. It was labor-intensive and in many cases dangerous.

It also required a thoughtful preparation. For the wise men, it made sense that the "scepter of Israel" would be found in Jerusalem, so that was their first destination. They went to where the King was. They arrived in Jerusalem asking, *"Where is He who has been born King of the Jews?"* Their question reached Herod, and of course, Herod, the king, was troubled. No one in Jerusalem knew anything about the birth of a royal child. Herod reached out to the priests and scribes, since they would know about this Jewish King. The religious men knew the Scriptures foretold Messiah would come from Bethlehem. Remember, this was their Anointed One, their Promised Redeemer. The One they had waited centuries to see. But they didn't follow. Though the Lord called to them through their knowledge of Scriptures, they chose not to go worship, or even acknowledge, their long-awaited King

Seeking the Lord requires us to leave our comfort zones of familiar beliefs and habits. It sometimes puts our reputations in jeopardy as people question why we choose to go a different direction from the crowd. When we come to Jesus we have to pack away the things that tie us to our old home- the one that's centered in self and the world- and move into a new dwelling place. This isn't a one-time thing for us. It's a process that takes a lifetime. For His part, in His great love for us and desire for us to come home to Him, God makes it clear to us where He is. We just have to surrender to His call.

Finally, the wise men worshipped Jesus. Seeing the star finally resting over Bethlehem the wise men *"rejoiced with exceeding great joy."* Surely they were relieved to have finally found the Messiah, but their rejoicing was much more than a sigh of relief. They were literally knocked off their feet by the weight of it. The presence of the Lord in our lives brings us exceeding, great joy- more joy than we could summon up on our own over life's circumstances. It's a kind of joy that weighs us down and causes us to fall to our knees, as the wise men did, to worship Jesus. This type of worship is not a simple kneel. It's a complete, face down, prostration- not in confession or repentance, not in supplication- but in worship. It's a physical response to being in the presence of the glory of God.

This kind of worship requires us to be completely vulnerable. It requires us to submit to the truth that our God is sovereign over us, and His power in our lives is greater than any control we might believe ourselves to have. Falling on our face before our Savior tells Him He is everything to us. And yet, this act of worship fills us with great peace- it puts things in our lives back in their right place. It puts us in the mindset of placing our treasures at the feet of our Savior- just as the wise men did. The offering of our gifts is integral to worship, but it's not out of compulsion. When true worship occurs in our hearts a new level of love, supernatural in nature, is bestowed on us (Gal. 5:22), and that love expresses itself in the giving of our gifts to the One we love.

Whether this Christmas season is your first encounter with the Christ child or whether the Christmas story has been a part of your story for a lifetime, the practice of seeking God is one that will never end until we are in Heaven with Him. Each day of our lives we are called to seek Him, we are led to seek Him in new places. Each new circumstance brings with it a new experience of His love, grace, mercy and kindness and a new opportunity to see a different facet of His glory. It's how this divine relationship unfolds. God is always drawing us home to Him. He knows that's the greatest longing in our hearts, because He put it there.

How is God drawing you to Himself today? What is the journey He is asking you to take? Take a few moments today to worship Him. Thank Him for always showing you exactly where to find Him.

# $\mathcal{D}ecember$ *15, 2023*

For the wise men, He sent a star. But sometimes, He doesn't. For the shepherds, God sent His heavenly messengers- the angels. For each of us, He has a unique way of calling us and leading us to Him, if we will take the time to pause and observe and ponder.

Over the past two years, for tens of thousands of immigrants and refugees from Afghanistan, God used the Taliban. As of January 2022, there were over 75,000 refugees from Afghanistan in the United States, arriving after the withdrawal of NATO troops in August of 2021, and the almost immediate takeover of Kabul by the Taliban. The refugees were relocated to various areas of the world, but let's just focus on the ones who are on American soil.

It's been a turbulent time for these people, many of them having left everything behind, including precious family members, in a little more than a moment's notice. Having reached the United States, they were then temporarily lodged in military housing until they could begin the processes and paperwork required to be established in our country. Then came the tasks to find permanent housing, transportation, employment, and education.

This was a historical moment, and from two different angles I found the timing of it to be interesting- at least to my limited perception. First, we have been reading for several years of the increasing number of Muslims who are coming to faith in Christ. Those who have been in ministry to Muslims have discovered that, even in the United States, crusade-like evangelism does not interest this population. The two things that seem to be effective are dreams and a relationship with a believer in Christ. Well, we obviously can't influence anyone to have a dream of Jesus, but we can show them the love of Jesus. Now, let me interject here that I don't know the percentages of these refugees who are Muslims, but it seems logical that many of them are, having come from an Islamic nation where only a fraction (.3%) of the citizens follow "other religions." Though August 2021 saw hundreds of thousands Afghans being resettled all over the world, it should be our prayer that those who came to America, a historically Christian nation, will have an opportunity to see the love Jesus has for them. This, however, will mean we as believers need to extend the hand of hospitality and welcome, build relationships, and live Gospel-colored lives.

The Afghan refugees didn't come to America with the purpose of finding Jesus- they were simply seeking safety and refuge. In this, we see the gracious hand of God leading the hopelessly lost to a place they could find the One Who can save their souls.

The Bible tells us that we are all sojourners here. The word sojourner means a stranger or foreigner, one who is temporarily living in a place where he is not a citizen. And in I Chronicles 29:15 David says this:

> *"For we are sojourners before You, and tenants, as all our fathers were; our days on the earth are like a shadow, and there is no hope."*

Paul puts that in perspective for us as believers in Philippians:

> *"For our citizenship is in heaven, from which also we eagerly wait for a Savior, the Lord Jesus Christ...."*

Though we are sojourners we know where we are going, and we know that we have a faithful Savior and Lord who is sitting on ready to bring us to our permanent home with Him. We are truly no longer homeless and hopeless- we have a place where we belong.

Today, thank God for your eternal, heavenly home. Even though it's easy sometimes to feel overwhelmed by the cares of this world and the temptations the enemy uses to lead you away, we have the blessed reminder of the Holy Baby in a manger who came to redeem us and secure our dwelling with Him. Spend time with Him today in worship and prayer.

Pray for God to use you to bring the hope of glory to those you who are lost. Ask the Holy Spirit to give you a sense of urgency to build relationships with people who need to know Jesus. Remember, they have an eternal destination as well, and without Jesus it's a place of darkness and horror. The Lord is literally bringing the lost to our doorstep- let's not waste the opportunities to show them His love.

COME TO BETHLEHEM AND SEE
HIM WHOSE BIRTH THE ANGELS SING
COME ADORE ON BENDED KNEE
CHRIST THE LORD, THE NEWBORN KING

# December 16, 2023

## ARE Y'ALL ALL RIGHT?

This morning, one of my coworkers sent a text to our office's group chat.

"House on fire. But everyone is out."

In the space of just a few minutes, their home, where they've lived less than six months, was gone. A total loss. But when I called him a few hours later and asked, "Are y'all all right?" He answered, in perfect 20-something fashion, "We're at Chick-Fil-A." I guess when you are experiencing the shock of having lost it all, you take your wife and three small children to get some of the "Lord's Chicken."

The pastor at our church often asks this same question, "Are y'all all right?" when he's delivering his sermons- a common preaching tactic to solicit an "amen" to one of those points that should have been a toe-stepper. Sometimes he gets a weak "amen." Often I hear only silence from his audience, but then, I sit in the back, and we tend to keep quiet.

One Sunday morning when he asked that question, I got a little distracted by it, and I hate to admit that I completely stopped listening to the man behind the podium (who, by the way, is a fascinating alliterator) and I just started pondering. Am I all right? Mornings are often physically difficult for me, and Sunday mornings especially so when I've spent the previous day catching up on chores. My back hurts my knees hurt my head is dizzy my eyes are dim. No, I thought. I am not "all right."

Then, I looked around the sanctuary at my church family.

I saw the woman whose child is battling addiction and mental illness. She is not all right.
I saw the man whose wife is dying of cancer.
He is not all right.
I saw the woman who had hired an aide to sit with her husband for an hour so he wouldn't wander off while she came to church.
She is not all right.
I saw the man who is just not making it financially, who is just one late paycheck away from living in his car.
He is not all right.

I saw the widows, the widowers, the parents and grandparents grieving the loss of a child, the cancer patients barely able to walk to the pew. All of us still standing to worship with all the strength we could muster, all cheerfully and faithfully giving within and beyond our means, all bowing our heads (because our knees no longer bend right to kneel) to pray silent prayers that only Jesus will ever hear, all listening to the words of a preacher and hoping to hear a message of encouragement that we can make it one more day.

No- none of us are "all right." We are sick, weak, bereaved, lonely, sad, struggling. We often pretend that things are all right because we so dearly wish they were. And let's face it, often we don't believe anyone really wants to hear our stories.

Though I won't ever recall the sermon preached on this particular Sunday, the preacher's question that morning was a sermon within a sermon.

See, the message of encouragement in that off-handed question that Sunday morning was this: in Heaven's economy, we are perfectly fine. From where Jesus stands, we are more than all right. We have reason to rejoice and be thankful in all things, for all things- because our Savior has come, and He is coming again one day soon. Isaiah writes:

> *And the ransomed of the Lord will return*
> *And come with joyful shouting in Zion,*
> *With everlasting joy upon their heads.*
> *They will find gladness and joy;*
> *And sorrow and sighing will flee away.*
> *(Isaiah 35:10)*

John writes:

> *Behold, the tabernacle of God is among men,*
> *And He will dwell among them and they shall be His people,*
> *And God Himself will be among them,*
> *And He will wipe away every tear from their eyes;*
> *And there will no longer be any death;*
> *There will no longer be any mourning, or crying, or pain;*
> *The first things have passed away.*
> *(Revelation 21:3-4)*

These two passages don't teach us sorrow and sighing don't exist. How could they flee if they weren't there? How could our Savior wipe away tears we've never cried? Or destroy pain we've never felt? These things right now are very real. But not for long.

As we sit here, in all of our "not-all-rightness," we are dwelling in the "first things" that John writes of. These hurts we feel today are all things that are going to pass away, they are going to be a *total loss*, so we can dwell in unhindered and everlasting joy and gladness in Zion, in the tabernacle, in the very presence of God.

Jesus, our Savior we celebrate in this season, our Messiah we are preparing our hearts to meet, made this our future. The good news of great joy those Christmas angels brought to the shepherds was more than a birth announcement- it was the news of redemption, the glory of God coming down to dwell with mankind, a taste of eternity.

Who do you know today who is not all right? A friend? A family member? A co-worker? Or maybe it's you. Open your Bible to the passages above and spend time reading and meditating on the blessing of the great hope we have of spending our eternity in the presence of God. Pray for those you know are hurting. Maybe take the time to call or visit and remind them of the good news of great joy.

Jesus came to make all of us all right. Thank Him for that today.

COME HOME TO A MANGER
COME HOME TO A STORY THAT'S STILL TRUE
COME HOME TO THE SAVIOR
WHO CAME DOWN FROM HEAVEN JUST FOR YOU
MATTHEW WEST

# *Week Three*

*And our eyes at last shall see Him*
*Through His own redeeming love.*
*For that Child so dear and gentle*
*Is our Lord in Heaven above.*

# December 17, 2023

## STIRRING THE GUMBO

I t was the night before Christmas Eve, and Aunt Betty's house was quietly snoring away while the crickets chirped outside in the warm South Mississippi December night. The Big Three (Mama and her two sisters) and their husbands were occupying the three bedrooms in the house. I was spending the night on the sofa in the living room, enjoying the sparkly flocked Christmas tree with its burden of ornaments in various shades of pink (because hey, it was the 90's). Right before bedtime, Aunt Betty said, "Ooooh! I've got to get the gumbo out." Yes, she said it just like that- exclamatory, as if she had just thought of it, when in reality we all knew it had been the only thing on her mind all evening. But the women in our family have a way of exclaiming over everything so that you never are quite sure if one of the uncles has set the chimney on fire or if the eggnog is running low. In our southern heritage, both situations are equally as critical. But I digress.

Upon Aunt Betty's gumbo exclamation, The Big Three marched in unison to the outside chest freezer. Most likely, they dragged one of the husbands along to do the heavy lifting, but all three sisters had to supervise. What was in that freezer was the biggest stock pot you could buy at the True Value on Main Street filled with pure gold- a frozen-solid brick of goodness that would transform into the centerpiece of our family's Christmas Eve dinner. The giant pot of frozen gumbo was placed on the back burner of the stove, and very vocal negotiations commenced between The Big Three over the correct temperature the pot of gold should ride out the night. Such "negotiations" were the constant back-drop of any meal preparations when The Big Three were together, so I'm sure I tuned them out, but soon it was settled and everyone retired to their bedrooms- the husbands in a sound, eggnog fueled night-night, The Big Three restless in their Vanity Fair night wear and silk and lace sleep bonnets.

Thawing that much frozen gumbo takes skill and attention. The thawing process has to happen low and slow, or the luxurious, silky, dark roux Aunt Betty agonized to make would turn into a burned mess and a scorched pot. We all knew that not everyone would sleep that night. Sure enough, all through the night, from my makeshift bed in the living room, I would hear the floor in the hallway creak as each one would take their turn sneaking into the kitchen to stir the gumbo, and I'm sure at least one of them (probably Eunice) made it a point to stub-bornly adjust the temperature. Aunt Betty probably adjusted it right back. All three of them most likely presumed they were the only one virtuous enough to sacrifice a night's sleep to tend to the most impor-tant meal of the year.

By morning, the house smelled of that wonderful and indescribable aroma of gumbo. Later in the day, pounds of crab, shrimp, and oysters would be added to the pot, then it would be ladled over fluffy white rice with stacks of Saltine crackers or hunks of garlic bread. Only then would it be Christmas Eve.

Stirring that gumbo is a perfect picture of the type of service that will be part of our lives in Heaven. I think we so often have the idea that in Heaven we will all be floating around God's throne on fluffy clouds, singing praise and worship songs. Or napping around the crystal sea eating exotic fruits with a lion curled up and purring by our side. Well, maybe. I don't know. We're talking about eternity and I have no idea what amazing things God has in store for us. But I do know this- knitted into our DNA, as part of His image expressed in us- is the desire and ability to be creative, to be productive, and to serve. In Heaven, where all our fallenness will no longer be an impediment, we will have unimaginable joy in creativity, productivity, and service.

Over and over in Scripture Jesus depicts Himself as a servant. One of the most profound expressions of this is in John 13. When He is preparing to have his final meal, the Passover supper, with His disciples, he kneels down and washes their feet. In Philippians 2 Paul writes that Christ took on the form of a servant. In fact, throughout His life He depicted the type of service He had created us to enjoy. These things were not burdensome or tedious to Him, and they aren't meant to be for us either. They are meant to bring us a sense of fulfillment.

When I was a child I memorized Psalm 100. The second verse tells us to *"Serve the Lord with gladness; come before Him with joyful singing."* Reading through the book of Revelation, it's amazing how many times the idea of serving the Lord is mentioned. It's a term that means to *do work*, and in some cases even carries the idea of being bound to someone for the purpose of serving.

Heaven is going to be a place where we serve God with great joy. Here on earth, even the idea of work carries with it the idea of burdensome labor. Our bodies grow tired and weary, and it seems our tasks are never complete before something else breaks. We are caught up in a multi-tasking society that is so overcome by stuff that has to be kept-up that we rarely feel that we can keep up. That won't be the case in Heaven. We will experience the joy we were meant to have in being industrious.

I like what David Jeremiah says about this:

*All of us will be serving in the fullest expression of the capacity God has given us and the giftedness with which He has blessed us. We will discover new gifts, new interests, and new pursuits. We will have new responsibilities and exercise positions of authority.... Someone has written, 'What will it be like to perform a task, to build and create, knowing that what we're doing will last forever and ever? What will it be like to always be gaining skills so that our best work will always be ahead of us....'"*

You probably know where I'm going with this, don't you? Heaven will be a place where the roux never burns, the cake never falls, you never run out of sugar, and onions don't make you cry. Right now, I imagine Heaven's kitchen is filled with the best cooks who have already gotten there before us. All of them have one hand on a hip, and the other stirring a big pot of something that will be going on the table when the Lamb calls us to supper.

Those of us who are here, waiting, anticipating the Lord's return, still have the call to serve. How can we do that during this season of the year?

We serve the Lord with our offerings of money, time, and other resources. But we also serve Him by serving others. In Jesus' teaching in Matthew 25 He says,

> *"Then the King will say to those on His right, 'Come, you who are blessed of My Father, inherit the kingdom prepared for you from the foundation of the world. For I was hungry, and you gave Me something to eat; I was thirsty, and you gave Me something to drink; I was a stranger and you invited Me in; naked, and you clothed Me; I was sick, and you visited Me; I was in prison, and you came to Me.' Then the righteous will answer Him, 'Lord, when did we see You hungry and feed you, or thirsty and give You something to drink? And when did we see You a stranger, and invite You in, or naked and clothe You? When did we see You sick or in prison and come to You?' The King will answer and say to them, 'Truly I say to you, to the extent that you did it to one of these brothers of Mine, even the least of them, you did it to Me."*

Yes, the expectation is that we will serve Him by serving one another. In fact, I believe there are people that He brings into our lives and across our paths who are brought there for us to practice this kind of humble compassion and lovingkindness and mercy and grace that He wants us to show.

The question today is simple- whom can you serve today, and how? If you ask the Lord to bring someone across your path, or to bring someone to your mind, He will do so. Ask Him to help you put your own comfort and agenda aside, and give you a generous and willing spirit.

As you step out in faith and obedience to serve, may your sacrifices bring delight to those around you, to yourself, and to your Savior.

# December 18, 2023

## THE GIFT OF THE (OTHER) MAGI

I f there's anything we have learned from O. Henry's short story, *The Gift of the Magi*, it's that communication is key this time of year. In the 1905 story, Della and Jim Young have very little money, but they want to buy special Christmas gifts for one another. Della presents Jim with a sturdy chain for his watch, which she bought with money she earned by selling her hair. Jim presents Della with a beautiful set of combs for her hair, which he bought after selling his watch. The story ends with each of them realizing the true gift is the sacrificial love shared between the two of them.

These days I find that Amazon Prime is a mixed blessing when it comes to gift giving. On the one hand, I think it's made gift-giving more difficult. We can, and do, order most anything we want and need. And why wait for Christmas when you can get it in two days any time of the year? What can we give to friends and family who already have purchased the latest and greatest of items for themselves? On the other hand, putting together a Christmas list is as simple as building an Amazon wish list with a few clicks- or, as in my case, I just find what I want and drop it in my mom's online shopping cart. Now, if you choose to try the cart-dropping method, make sure the person knows what's yours when the packages are dropped off at your house!

Now, yes, I know that there's this whole new philosophy that "Christmas is not about presents, it's about presence." And as much as I'd like to be noble and "spiritual" about it, on Christmas morning, I will unashamedly admit, I want to be exchanging presents with everyone who is present. I want to present my family and friends with beautifully wrapped boxes with well-thought out gifts. And I want to have presents to open, too. To me, a good gift is one that delights the one receiving it- like the yodeling pickle that I picked out for a friend last year. No, it's not the gift for everyone, but it definitely brought some joy and laughter at our gift exchange. The giving and receiving of gifts is all about blessing. It is a blessing to receive a gift, but it's also a blessing to give. Why wouldn't we want to do that?

Which brings me to my next thought- choosing the best gift requires us to know the recipient. These best gifts come out of really thinking about the person, not in that place of slightly panicked desperation of "I have no idea what to get her!" that comes more from a sense of obligation rather than from a sense of wanting to bless someone else. And honestly, the inspiration for the best gifts doesn't come during a Christmas shopping excursion. Instead, it comes as we think about and pray for our loved ones throughout the year. It comes as we talk with one another and listen to the things that bring joy or warmth to a person's life. We notice little things about them as we spend time with them, and as we talk about things that bring them comfort or fulfillment.

There's so much about the giving of gifts in Scripture it's hard to even begin to address it in this short space. I suppose, though, that one of the best verses about gifts can be found in James 1:17-18:

> *Every good thing given and every perfect gift is from above, coming down from the Father of lights, with whom there is no variation or shifting shadow. In the exercise of His will He brought us forth by the word of truth, so that we would be a kind of first fruits among His creatures.*

In verse 17, we find two different words for "gift." The first, "every good thing given," refers to the act of giving, while the second, "gift," refers to the gift itself. John MacArthur points out that everything associated with God's giving is adequate, complete, and beneficial. In verse 18 is an interesting thought about giving. The idea that we are *a kind of first fruits*, refers to that part of the harvest that God's people were instructed to give as an offering to Him (Proverbs 3:9-10). We are to give Him the best of ourselves. In this context though, there's another connotation that shines a bright light on why those first fruits were such an important offering.

For the farmer, giving God the first and best of his crops, was purely an act of faith. To give the best as an offering to God, rather than as securing a profit, exhibited that God could be completely trusted to provide an even greater harvest. In the lives of believers, the first fruits are produced by the Holy Spirit as an indication that we have the hope of a greater harvest within us- the harvest of eternal life. In Romans 8:23, Paul tells us that those first fruits of the Spirit are so deeply rooted in us, that we are groaning as we wait for *"our adoption as sons, the redemption of our body."*

Just like children during Christmas- watching that pile of gifts under the tree growing every day of December until they can hardly contain their excitement- our anticipation grows as the days grow closer and closer to the return of Christ. As we wait for that ultimate Christmas Day, we are blessed to experience all of God's perfect gifts as He expresses His limitless love, grace, and mercy toward us.

But this gift giving is not one sided. The writer of Hebrews tells us to *"continually offer up a sacrifice of praise to God, that is, the fruit of lips that give thanks to His name. And do not neglect doing good and sharing, for with such sacrifices God is pleased."* Psalm 22:3 tells us that God inhabits the praises of His people- He is present, drawing near to us, as we offer to Him our sacrifices of praise. When we take the time to know our Savior and our God, when we spend time talking with Him, listening to His voice as we read and reflect on His Word, we begin to understand better how we can honor Him and praise Him. We begin to find the posture of praise coming naturally for us as we sense His presence in more profound ways every day. And we begin to feel the excitement in our souls build as we anticipate and prepare our hearts to meet Him face to face.

Today, spend some moments simply praising God. It may feel awkward to you, and it may be difficult during those times when you may not feel like praising Him; remember, this is a "sacrifice" of praise. Honor Him by spending time in His presence, expressing your love and thanksgiving to Him. See what changes in your life when you make the space in your day to praise Him. Then, think about someone you can bless today. Who can you share a simple, but special gift with during this time of year that will bring a great blessing to the both of you?

# December 19, 2023

## THE ROYAL STANDARD

On Thursday, September 8, 2022, Queen Elizabeth II died in Scotland at Balmoral Castle. She was 96 years old, and according to her death certificate, the cause of her death was old age. She was the longest reigning British monarch, and was very much beloved by people around the world. Her life exemplified service, and even up until the final days of her life, she was serving; her last public statement was one of condolences for the victims of a brutal crime in Canada. All over the world, flags flew at half-mast in mourning the loss of this great leader. But in Britain, though other flags would be lowered, the Royal Standard would not be half-masted. On the afternoon of September 8, the Royal Standard was flying at Balmoral Castle to indicate the Queen was in residence. Upon her death around 3:00 PM, that flag was lowered briefly, then promptly raised once more. This flag will never be flown at half mast, because there will always be a Sovereign on the throne.

The Royal Standard represents the Sovereign and the United Kingdom. For Queen Elizabeth the Standard was very special as it was a reminder to her of the realm she served, which included England, Scotland, and Ireland. This striking flag of crimson and gold and blue is flown on buildings and vehicles that indicates the monarch, now King Charles III, is present.

The Christmas story, so beloved by all of us, is the story of a King who also wanted His presence known to His people. Since the tragic act of disobedience in the Garden of Eden, God has been announcing the arrival of the Messiah- the one who would come and save His people from our sin. Through prophecies, dreams and visions, the miraculous virgin birth, the star, the angels- it couldn't have been more clear that our God desired to dwell with us, and be present among us.

The Israelites always knew God's presence was with them because His glory would rest over the tabernacle and the temple. We know this as His *shekinah* glory, with the word *shekinah* meaning *a dwelling*. We read throughout the Old Testament about God's glory leading His people through the wilderness, of His glory filling the temple. We read of the great power and unapproachableness of His glory. But then there He was- a helpless newborn, lying in a manger, surrounded by shepherds- men who were considered unclean and not fit to enter the presence of the glorious God. But there they were, worshipping Him in the straw, sweaty and smelly with empty hands that had not been washed all night- the sheep that should have been offered up to this King having been left out on the hillside.

This Baby was the way that God would now show His people that His heart is filled with great love for us. Because just as He loves us with all His power and might and glory, He loves us with a sweet tenderness and joy that sometimes we may tend to forget about. Zephaniah wrote about it:

> *The Lord your God is in your midst, a victorious warrior. He will exult over you with joy,*
> *He will be quiet in His love, He will rejoice over you with shouts of joy.*
> (Zephaniah 3:17)

He delights in us. He delights in being with us so much that He chose to come and make His home among us so that we could one day be at home for eternity with Him. How reassuring it is, on these days that are growing so dark and filled with hardship, to know He is even now preparing that home for us.

Throughout Scripture, Old and New Testament alike, we read the words that thrill our souls- words that speak of the Heaven He is preparing for us, that dwelling place where we can live with Him and one another for eternity in the place always intended to be our home. In the last verse of the book of Ezekiel is a beautiful verse of Scripture: ... *and the name of the city from that day shall be "YHWH Shammah- The Lord is there."* (Ezekiel 48:35) This was a beautiful prophecy for Israel, who had experienced the departure of the glory of God from the temple. But God is a covenant-keeping God, and this little verse was full of life-giving hope- the promise of a city called YHWH Shammah.

Will there be a Royal Standard flying over that city? Song of Solomon 2:4 tells us this:

> *"He has brought me to His banquet hall, and His banner over me is love."*

There are so many expressions over the course of our days that remind us we are living under this banner of our Lord's love. His presence in our lives, the redemption He has accomplished for us, His drawing us to Him, our promised future home, all speak to the depth of the love He has for us. Though we can sort of experience that love in the here and now, I suppose we won't fully experience it until are with Him, sitting across the table from Him, walking hand in hand with Him. Not until we experience dwelling in that city called *YHWH Shammah* will we really know what His love for us is truly like. Now, we can read it on the page, and His Spirit can whisper it into our hearts. But then, we will hear it from His own voice and see it in His eyes.

What is our response today to knowing that we dwell under this Royal Standard of the love of God? I believe He made it clear that our response, our Royal Standard is three-fold- love God, obey God, love one another.

First:

*You shall love the Lord your God with all your heart, and with all your soul, and with all your mind.*
(Matthew 22:37)

Second:
*If you love Me, you will keep My commandments.*
(John 14:15)

Third:
*This is My commandment, that you love one another, just as I have loved you.*
(John 15:12)

How can you express your love for God today? Is there a place in your heart, your life, or your mind that you have closed off from Him? Confess that today and ask for His grace to repent and change. Is there a place of disobedience in your life? Today is the day to get that right. Finally consider how Jesus has loved you- how He laid down His life for you. How can you show your love to Him today?

# December 20, 2023

T.S. Eliot wrote,
"What life have you if you have not life together?
There is no life that is not in community,
And no community not lived in praise of God."

Those words are profound and touching, but read the rest of the stanza of this section of "Choruses from the Rock," and you will see that Eliot's words were in the context of describing a world where self-centered materialism and a drive for always having more make that community seem out of reach. He writes, "And no man knows or cares who is his neighbour, Unless his neighbour makes too much disturbance."

The truth is we were created for community, and our community should be lived in praise and worship of God. But the other side of that truth is the world we live in often leaves us feeling lonely and isolated. Even living and working in close proximity to others we can often feel very much alone. During the holiday season, as friends and families gather to celebrate Thanksgiving and Christmas, the lonely feel even more alone and often spend those joyous days in bittersweet grief.

Joanne Huist Smith experienced such loneliness during Christmastime in 1999. In her book, *The 13th Gift: A True Story of a Christmas Miracle,* she writes how she had spent her life grasping the "five golden rings" of her husband, her three children (then ages 10, 12, and 17), and her comfortable home. Then, her husband died unexpectedly shortly before Christmas and her world was shattered. The last thing she wanted that year was Christmas. One hurried morning, 13 days before Christmas, as Joanne and her children were heading out to school and work, they opened the front door to find a poinsettia on the doorstep. Along with the plant was a homemade Christmas card that read, "On the first day of Christmas your true friends give to you, one Poinsettia for all of you."

Joanne and the kids were mystified- who could the true friends be? She wrote, "Right now, I don't feel as if we have any friends. Telephone calls to chat and make plans for weekend gatherings have stopped. There are no Christmas cards in our mailbox, only bills." But over the next weeks leading up to Christmas, every day another gift arrived, each one accompanied by a hand made card that included the lyrics to "The Twelve Days of Christmas" that had been rewritten to go along with the gift. The gifts were not extravagant- wrapping paper, candles, notecards. But they were significant in that not a day was missed, and they were thoughtful. The *True Friends* seemed to understand that things usually commonplace at Christmastime might be overlooked or forgotten by the newly bereaved. They understood because they had been there once, too. And, the time and effort the *True Friends* invested in their Yuletide project, especially to maintain the mystery when Joanne and her kids decided to catch them in the act, gave a sense of playfulness to the season for the family. But it was the simple act of being remembered by people who saw what they were going through and who decided to bring Christmas to a home that most likely would've had none that year- that itself was the 13th gift.

When Jesus was asked by the scribe in the Temple what the greatest commandment is, He responded, *"You shall love the Lord your God with all your heart, and with all your soul, and with all your mind."* But before the scribe could respond, Jesus continued, *"The second is like it, 'You shall love your neighbor as yourself.'"* Sometimes in reading this verse, we get things backwards. We create a between-the-lines commandment of sorts to love ourselves first. The mistaken thought is that we can't love others if we don't first love ourselves. Well, that is not what Jesus was saying here.

We are instructed to love God. We are instructed to love our neighbors. These are commands, not touchy-feely outpourings of emotional affirmations. Think about the amount of money (heart), time (soul), and thought (mind) that goes into the self-care industry these days. In reality, by obeying these commands to love God and love others we find the care that our souls really need, and in doing so, we also lift up those around us who are struggling. That place of struggle is familiar to all of us, so we should know what people need in those times. We should know that a woman who has lost her husband at Thanksgiving might forget to buy the Christmas ham, or that a family who has recently lost all their belongings in a fire might not prioritize a Christmas tree this year. A ham, a tree- such simple things we can do to show that we care for their souls.

As I consider the work of Advent- the work of examining my heart, my soul, and my mind- if I am truly loving my Lord, my God, with all of myself, one of the evidences will be how well I am loving my neighbor. There should be a direct correlation between those two. My love for Jesus should overflow into genuine, compassionate love for the people He brings into my life, whether those people are there for a season or for a lifetime. By keeping my gaze on my Savior I am more able to see His image in the faces of others, and I can love them in obedience to this second great commandment. I can be the *true friend* I am called to be as a follower of Jesus.

Advent reminds us that we have just a few short days to get this right. We can't forget why we observe this time of year- to draw closer to our Savior as time draws us closer to His return for us. While He tarries, it is our privilege and responsibility to allow Him to use us to bring hope, peace, love, and joy into the lives of our neighbors. We people are messy and complicated and often difficult to love- but let's take the initiative today to love someone anyway.

What about you? What are some ways your love for God overflows in love for your neighbor? Joanne's family wasn't the first or the last recipients of the *True Friends'* gifts. It seems they show up every year where they find people, within their reach, who need such support during the holidays. We all can't pull off schemes like they do, but as you've read Joanne's story, have you thought of someone in your life you can show that kind of love to? How will you do that today?

It's the smile on a man who has finally found hope
It's the tears of a mother whose child has come home
It's the joy that we feel and the love that we share
There's a little bit of Heaven everywhere
It's the grace that we show to a world that needs hope
It's giving our lives knowing they're not our own
It's the joy that we feel and the love that we share
There's a little bit of Heaven everywhere
Francesca Battistelli

<h1>December 21, 2023</h1>

## THE GRINCH

It was always my least favorite Christmas cartoon. I never felt like the few minutes of the "good" Grinch really gave me any reason to believe he wouldn't go back to his "bad" Grinch ways. Maybe I didn't believe he had completely made up for all the bad he had done. The thing is, I just didn't trust the guy. At the end, when he gives back all the Christmas he had stolen and has that emotional moment with Cindy Lou Who, the story says that his heart grew three whole sizes bigger. Well, in my research, that kind of rapid cardiac growth is indicative of the physiology of the Burmese python. Yeah, a snake.

Though the Grinch is a fictional character, a product of Dr. Seuss's imagination, the author revealed that he didn't have to work too hard to create the fuzzy green beast. One December 26, when he was 53 years old, he was brushing his teeth and found the Grinch in the mirror. In a 1957 interview he confessed that morning he'd realized either something was wrong with Christmas, or something was wrong with him. So, he wrote the story to see if he could regain what was lost.

Most all of us have been on one side or the other of Grinchiness. There's a lady I am vaguely acquainted with in my church who responds to my smiles and "Good mornings" with an icy glare that makes me think she'd yank the tinsel off my tree if she could. I'm not sure why. Like Dr.

Suess said regarding the Grinch, I don't quite know the reason for her grudge. I just keep smiling. I'd like to ask her forgiveness for whatever I've done to offend her, but so far I've only been granted an audience with her back.

I realize, if I had to assemble an apology-line of all the people I have offended with missteps or thoughtless words it would take more time than any of us likely have left on this earth. Knowing my carelessness, I do my best to keep short accounts with God and with others and try to carefully weigh my words before I speak. I often fail, sadly. Our relationships with one another are too precious to mess up with foolishness, but unforunately it's taken many of us a really long time to figure that out.

Psalm 120:6 reads, *"Too long has my soul had its dwelling with those who hate peace,"* and I get that. The context of the entire chapter, I think, is about taking care with our own words, and being an instrument of peace in the place where God has planted us. In this case, it seems the psalmist was actually dwelling in a land of mainly unbelieving people- and I think we can all relate to that.

Psalm 120 is the first of the Psalms of Ascent, which were a group of Psalms (120-134) the Jewish people would sing when traveling to Jerusalem for the three feasts, or festivals, required by the Law. To say they were "required" sounds binding and tedious. But that's our modern tendency to put the emphasis in the wrong place. The emphasis should be on "feasts" or "festivals." These were times of celebration when God's people would gather in fellowship to be encouraged by and with one another and experience spiritual renewal- even though they were scattered and living in places far from Zion- the city associated with God's presence. Though this first Psalm expressed a longing for God's presence and a longing for peace, there's an underlying joy knowing that they are traveling together to that place where they will celebrate all of God's help and provision.

Together- that is key. There is a great sense of togetherness when we consider God's dwelling with us. I like how the writer of Hebrews breaks down the importance of this in chapter 10. First, in verses 19-22 he reminds us of our togetherness with God:

*Therefore brethren, since we have confidence to enter the holy place by the blood of Jesus, by a new and living way which He inaugurated for us through the veil, that is, His flesh, and since we have a great priest over the house of God, let us draw near with a sincere heart in full assurance of faith, having our hearts sprinkled clean from an evil conscience and our bodies washed with pure water.*

Here the writer reminds us that, because of Jesus's sacrifice for us, we can enter into the very presence of God- which we literally did when Jesus came to earth as a baby and walked among us, and we still do as we walk in step with His Spirit living within us. When He gave His life for us, Jesus made it possible for us to be together with God.

The Hebrews writer goes on to emphasize how important it is for us to be together with other believers. In verses 24-25 he writes:

*And let us consider how to stimulate one another to love and good deeds, not forsaking our own assembling together, as is the habit of some, but encouraging one another; and all the more as you see the day drawing near.*

The Hebrew believers had experienced persecution, and were apparently anticipating more to come. It was so important for them to stay close together for support and encouragement, and to keep one another from drifting (or even running) away from their faith when the days got difficult.

And we need this connection to one another, too. As members of the body of Christ, the Church, we are not meant to distance ourselves from one another for any reason. We are instructed to be forgiving and longsuffering with each other. And look, the fact there are so many passages in Scripture talking about how we're supposed to bear with each other shows we are prone to messing up when it comes to our relationships. The world we live in today makes it so easy to take issue with each other and keep our bitter little grudges against each other polished as thoroughly as if they're jewels.

When Jesus was born in Bethlehem the message the angels gave was a message of *peace.* Peace with God, and peace with man. God truly wants us to be people of peace, as He is a God of peace. When we dwell within the veil, fully in His presence, we will find deep and true fellowship with others who are worshiping there. In that place, the pettiness of our offenses and our grudges will disappear- we'll see they just don't matter. We'll see what matters is the love and care we show to one another, the encouragement we provide within the body of Christ to those who are struggling and hurting. We'll begin to see one another the way God sees us- dearly loved and worthy of forgiving. We'll begin to see how important celebrating together is, just like God instructed His people long ago. And we'll make opportunities to encourage one another.

Like those ancient Jews, traveling up to Jerusalem, we are all on a journey to Heaven. Let's be good traveling companions for those who are on this road with us.

Are you at peace today with the people in your life? Maybe you can think of someone in your life you should forgive, or maybe you can think of someone you should celebrate with, or encourage. Pray for the grace to reach out to someone today, and pray that as you act in obedience, God will fill your heart with peace.

# December 22, 2023

## THE REJECTS

Yesterday I baked 18 dozen cookies for a friend's book signing event. I measured, mixed, and scooped the dough into carefully arranged lines on my cookie sheets, slid the pans into the oven, set the timer, and went on about my business for the next 9 to 11 minutes. Everything was fine. I mean, it's cookies- it's not national security. Until it wasn't fine.

Midway through, on about dozen #8, the timer went off at the 9 minute mark. I grabbed my pot-holders and opened the oven to find my carefully scooped pan of 20 cookies had oozed into a single somewhat dark COOKIE. That wouldn't do. Sticking the next pan into the oven, I surveyed the COOKIE to see if I could salvage at least one or two presentable cookies. I used my spatula as a chisel to try to sculpt a normal cookie from the mess- only to discover that the dough had bonded with the non-stick, and cooking spray coated for extra insurance, surface of the pan.

Disappointed, I turned my spatula over and began to scrape the COOKIE off the pan in segments I like to refer to as The Rejects. The Rejects are baking projects that don't turn out in good enough condition to be presented at social affairs but are still perfectly edible and very tasty. For as long as I can remember, The Rejects would be packaged up and set aside for George Starr, the lover of all things sweet. He especially loved The Rejects even when Alzheimer's had taken most of him away from us. But George Starr went to heaven a couple of months ago, so with a mixture of sorrow for our loss and gladness for his healing, I scraped The Rejects into the trash.

Around the holidays, George always knew he could count on me to keep him stocked in rejected baking and candy-making projects. Along with his annual German Chocolate Cake he knew he would get a good selection of broken and semi-charred baked goods and chocolate covered somethings that were not aesthetically pleasing enough for a formal tin-gift. He always greeted these rejects with as much enthusiasm as if they were professionally made and wrapped in fancy tinsel instead of zip-lock bags. Why? Because what was in those zip-lock bags tasted every bit as good as what was in the fancy wrappers and tins.

And you know, I kind of feel that's the way God greets us when we come to Him. We are charred, broken- inside and out. No matter how hard we try to make ourselves appealing by trying to be good and look good- God sees what's really in our hearts. He sees the selfishness, the pride, the envy, the anger, the bitterness. He knows the secret thoughts we think and hears the words we only utter in hushed whispers.

But God sees even deeper than that. In each one of us He sees a precious, intricately designed being- fearfully and wonderfully made by His very own hands and brought to life by His very own breath. Like a sculptor sees a masterpiece in a lump of clay, God sees in you and me a person dearly loved by His Father's heart, and a person worthy of the deepest compassion and unfathomable grace that would be required to reunite us with Him. Isaiah wrote that *"If He would render Himself as a guilt offering, He will see His offspring."* (Isaiah 53:10). Our Father loves us- loves you- that much. He loves you enough to sacrifice His own Son so that you can be redeemed. In Romans 5:6-8 we read:

*For while we were still helpless, at the right time Christ died for the ungodly. For one will hardly die for a righteous man; though perhaps for the good man someone would dare even to die. But*

*God demonstrates His own love toward us, in that while we were yet sinners, Christ died for us.*

In this scenario, in our very reality, we were The Rejects, broken and charred by sin, with no way to put ourselves right. He couldn't wait for us to be good enough to secure our own atonement- because we never would be good enough. Nothing we could do- no good works or good choices or good behavior- could ever, can ever, fix what was wrong. Only Jesus could do that. Only Jesus did.

And so, He tells us to come to Him in Matthew 11:28-30:

*Come to Me, all who are weary and heavy-laden, and I will give you rest. Take My yoke upon you and learn from Me, for I am gentle and humble in heart, and You will find rest for your souls. For My yoke is easy and My burden is light.*

Though we like to think of this passage when we are tired from the difficulties of life, what Jesus was specifically talking about here was the burden to meet an impossible religious performance standard that was placed on people by the Pharisees, who spoke of taking on the "yoke of Torah," or the lifestyle of performing according to Rabbinic teaching- which when seen together was completely unattainable. These burdens were heavy, and the religious leaders offered the people no help or mercy.

Jesus wanted the people to know He is different. Yes, He also has a yoke, but as Matthew Henry has written, it is a yoke that's lined with love. He also expects us to carry the burden of obedience and submission to His authority. But He, Himself, is different. His heart is gentle and humble, and Who He is makes the burdens we carry with Him easy and light. One commentator has said that those who come to Jesus "find a challenging yoke, but also a compassionate Savior who encourages, loves, forgives, restores, strengthens, and saves."

Why such a difference between the demands of the religious leaders and those of Christ? Simply because the Pharisees didn't believe Jesus was the Messiah. They didn't understand that there was a better way. They knew there was a promise of a new covenant, because they knew the Scripture from Jeremiah 31 that says,

> *"Behold, days are coming," declares the Lord, "when I will make a new covenant with the house of Israel and with the house of Judah.... I will put My law within them and on their heart I will write it; and I will be their God, and they shall be My people. They will not teach again, each man his neighbor and each man his brother, saying, 'Know the Lord,' for they will all know Me, from the least of them to the greatest of them," declares the Lord, "for I will forgive their iniquity, and their sin I will remember no more."*

But the Pharisees were so blinded by their own self-righteousness that they completely overlooked the Messiah, the one Who would usher in, by His own blood, this new covenant.

This new covenant means that He forgives our sins because He has atoned for them and provided the way, the only way, for us to be made right with God. He refuses to remember our sin. Also, He gives us His Holy Spirit, Who witnesses to our spirits, so our eyes can be opened to Him. He gives us the faith to trust our sins are truly forgiven- thrown completely away.

He dispatches our sins as far as the east is from the west, and He- the One we have offended by our unrighteousness- refuses to remember them.

*He* does that, not us; and He does so much more:
*He* restores the health and heals the wounds of the outcasts (Jeremiah 30:17).
*He* intercedes for us when we don't have the words to pray. (Romans 8:26)
*He* causes all things to work together for good for us. (Romans 8:28)
*He* chooses us. (John 15:16)
*He* makes all things possible. (Matthew 19:26)
*He* will be the one who will wipe away every tear. (Revelation 21:4)

*He* will make all things, including you and me, new. (Revelation 21:5)
*He* is making a home for us in Heaven. (John 14:2)

Do you see? *He* does it all. Not us- *only Him*. This is what true freedom in Christ looks like. We come to Him as rejects, outcasts. He makes us accepted and whole. And what's our part?

We love Him.
We come to Him.
We submit to Him in faith and obedience.

It isn't always easy because until we arrive in Heaven, there will always be a part of us that's a little bit charred and a little bit broken. But we can be assured that even in the difficulties, and even in those moments we fail, we are still dearly loved. He has chosen to dwell with us, to be our Immanuel, and because of this, we are no longer Rejects.

Maybe there are times in your life when you feel you just don't measure up. I hope you will be encouraged today by the truth that your sins are forgiven, you are accepted in Christ, and you are dearly loved. Maybe today is the day you will renew your faith in Jesus, or maybe you will trust Him for your salvation for the first time. As we grow closer each day to Christmas, I pray your joy in anticipation of Christ's return will sustain you no matter what you are facing. Thank Him today for His unfathomable grace and measureless love that has secured your eternal home in Heaven.

## LET THE STABLE STILL ASTONISH: BY LESLIE LEYLAND FIELDS

*Let the stable still astonish:*
*Straw-dirt floor, dull eyes,*
*Dusty flanks of donkeys, oxen;*
*Crumbling, crooked walls;*
*No bed to carry that pain,*
*And then, the child,*
*Rag-wrapped, laid to cry*
*In a trough.*

*Who would have chosen this?*
*Who would have said, "Yes,*
*Let the God of all the heavens and earth*
*Be born here, in this place."?*

*Who but the same God*
*Who stands in the darker, fouler rooms of our hearts*
*And says, "Yes, let the God*
*Of heaven and earth*
*Be born here----*

*In this place."*

# December 23, 2023

## LET THE STABLE STILL ASTONISH

This poem by Leslie Leyland Fields has been one of my favorites for many years. Fields has brilliantly crafted the image of the newborn Christ child being born in a place animals are tended, being laid in a feeding trough in cloths most likely used for lambs. Yes, how unlikely for a child to be born there. But how astonishing that our God would choose this place for the Messiah's birth- a God whose law required His people to maintain strict standards of washing and cleanliness.

This picture of Jesus' birthplace says a lot to me about the place He would choose for His earthly home. He could have been born in any number of beautiful places earth has to offer- a palace with a breathtaking mountain vista, or an equally beautiful view of a seashore. In His sovereignty, He could have even ordained a vacancy in that inn and had at least a clean bed for His birth.

But a stable is what He chose. Such a lowly place. But the night He came from Heaven, even that stable was filled with glory.

As Fields' poem goes on to describe, the truth that Jesus chose the stable gives me great hope. My heart does not always offer the most beautiful of views. My heart is often lowly, filled with discouragement and sadness, with ugliness, with sin. My heart is most definitely darker and fouler than that stable. And yet a holy and righteous Savior has chosen my heart as His dwelling place? Astonishing. Utterly astonishing.

I don't believe, however, that it's necessary for me to defend the point here that Christ seeks out the outcasts, the lowly, and yes, even the vilest of sinners. We are all part of "the world" spoken of in John 3:16, the world that "God so loved," as stated by Christ, God Incarnate. Yes, He will dwell in you and me, and in everyone who accepts the free gift of faith He offers us.

How exactly does this happen? How does He dwell in us? What does it mean?

In John 14:23, Jesus tells His disciples: *"If anyone loves Me, he will keep My word; and My Father will love him, and We will come to him and make Our abode with him."* I can't help but be reminded of Mary. The angel explained to Mary that she would conceive when the Holy Spirit would come upon her, and she would be overshadowed by the power of the Most High (Luke 1:35). Twice in Luke 2 we see Mary in deep wonder, treasuring everything she was learning about her Son- loving Him as her child, but also loving Him as her Messiah.

It's only by the Lord dwelling in us that we know Him. But He isn't just a roommate to share the rent and the utility bills. He dwells with us so we can have an ever deepening intimate relationship with Him. The expanding love and obedience that is evidence of our faith will grow deeper and stronger as we seek Him in His Word.

Sometimes those of us who have been believers for a long time can find we've adopted what I call "church people" habits and preferences. We behave a certain way and prefer certain things because we're church attenders and much of our social interaction revolves around the church. We listen to Christian radio. We try to watch all the Christian movies that come out. We have a Bible app on our phones that sends us a verse to think about every day. Are these things evidences that Jesus has made His home with me? Or is that me, trying to live a so-called Christian life?

In Paul's letter to the Corinthian church we read that we are to test ourselves to see if we are in the faith. Paul writes, *"Examine yourselves! Or do you not recognize this about yourselves, that Jesus Christ is in you- unless indeed you fail the test?"* (2 Corinthians 13:5) In other words, are you growing in grace and increasing in holiness? This is what happens when Christ dwells in you: He doesn't just change what you do- He changes who you are. Your part is to respond in obedience.

There are many ways we should examine ourselves. I heard a sermon recently where a pastor was talking about taking our spiritual temperature. He used the example of when we go to the doctor the first thing they do is take our temperature by putting a thermometer under our tongue. He said if we want to take our spiritual temperature, the tongue is the first place we should check. Our thoughts and our words when someone hurts us is a good indicator of whether we are growing in grace and increasing in holiness- whether we are living in our flesh, or whether Jesus is truly living in us and through us. The psalmist wrote, *"Holiness befits Your house, O Lord, forevermore."* (Psalm 93:5) When Jesus is living in us, we will experience His holiness in our lives.

In John 15:1-11, Jesus talks with His disciples about what it means to abide with Him. The word picture He gives them is that of a vine with branches loaded with fruit. He is the vine, and we are the branches, connected to Him through love and obedience. In this object lesson, the life of the vine flows through those branches. So we can say then that Jesus' life flows through us when we love and obey Him. It's expected that Jesus' disciples will bear fruit, but this can't be done in our own power- it is a result of His life flowing through us. (John 15:5) When His life flows through us, His desires become our desires and this yields a life of answered prayer. (John 15:7) When His life flows through us, we will love and be loved- just as He loves and is loved by God. (John 15:10) When His life flows through us, His joy becomes our joy. (John 15:11)

At times I find I take for granted Christ's presence in my heart. I struggle through issues when I should trust Him, or I get discouraged and disheartened when I see situations from my human perspective instead of seeing them through His. Do you find this to be true in your life? Paul's prayer in Ephesians 3:16-21 is one that I would like to leave you with today.

> *...that He would grant you, according to the riches of His glory, to be strengthened with power through His Spirit in the inner man, so that Christ may dwell in your hearts through faith; and that you, being rooted and grounded in love, may be able to comprehend with all the saints what is the breadth and length and height and depth, and to know the love of Christ which surpasses knowledge, that you may be filled up to all the fullness of God. Now to Him who is able to do far more abundantly beyond all that we ask or think, according to the power that works within us, to Him be the glory in the church and in Christ Jesus to all generations forever and ever. Amen.*

All the fullness of God residing in this fouler and darker room of my heart? How could He choose this? Why would He choose any of us as His dwelling place? Astonishing, amazing grace, indeed.

Do you struggle to comprehend the kind of love that surpasses knowledge? You can experience the fullness of it, and live in faith in the One who lives in you. Remember He didn't choose you because of your goodness, He chose you because of His own goodness. And just like the stable glowed with the glory of God's presence on the night Jesus came to earth, your heart- His home, His temple- can reflect His glory, too.

## DWELLING WITH HIM TODAY

Tomorrow is Christmas Eve. Most likely it's a busy day at your house. If you're reading this in the morning, maybe you're looking forward to a long day of traveling, cooking, shopping, and wrapping. If you're reading this in the evening, maybe you're tired from having done all those things! Whichever may be the case, today, I'd like you to set aside this book, and pick up His book- the Bible. Find a quiet place and a quiet moment and read His story. But don't just read the words. Hear His Spirit. Let yourself be transported in your heart back to the time and the place your Savior was born. Try to imagine the glory of God illuminating that stable, His infant cries mingling with the sounds of the animals. Dwell with Him in the words in your Bible, and let Him minister peace and joy to your heart.

Read:
Matthew 1:18-2:12
Luke 2:1-20
John 1:1-14
Revelation 21:1-8
Revelation 22:1-7

BORN THY PEOPLE TO DELIVER
BORN A CHILD AND YET A KING
BORN TO REIGN IN US FOREVER
NOW THY GRACIOUS KINGDOM BRING
BY THINE OWN ETERNAL SPIRIT
RULE IN ALL OUR HEARTS ALONE
BY THINE ALL SUFFICIENT MERIT
RAISE US TO THY GLORIOUS THRONE.

# Christmas

*And in His temple everything says, "Glory!"*
*Psalm 29:9b*

# December 24, 2023

I t was a glorious night. But it didn't start out that way. It started out the way all the other night shifts did- going through all the motions of setting up the camp to guard the flock through the night. There were no comforts of home to be had out in the fields. These men were serious about their work. They would get the job done.

It was taxing work- each lamb was precious and each one had to be protected from danger. The same dangers that threatened the lambs also threatened the shepherds. There was no room for distraction from their task. These men were serious about their jobs.

They were prepared for most anything. They had anticipated wild animals and all precautions had been taken. They had anticipated cold air, parasites, injuries- all of these things they had faced before and they were ready to face again.

They had never in their wildest dreams imagined an angel of the Lord- but that was exactly what they encountered tonight. And they were terrified. Momentarily forgetting their sheep, they cowered first in fear, and then knelt in reverence. And there on that hillside they received the good news of great joy from this heavenly messenger.

There was yet more unexpectedness to the night when the multitude of the heavenly host appeared all around them. This angel host was along the lines of a military regiment, and was likely made up of so very many angels- too many to even be counted. Maybe their presence was to provide protection to the holy family- Mary and Joseph- as the God of Heaven burst forth into humanity that night. Perhaps they came as protection for the helpless new born, incarnate King of Kings.

But in this moment, the angels were there to worship God. After all, God was right there, just a few miles away, lying in a manger, transformed through the miracle of the virgin birth into the form of a baby. This miracle, a part of the unfolding of God's plan to dwell with man, was beyond comprehension.

Just like the shepherds and the angels, it's best for us to adopt the same response to Christ's birth- worship. To those shepherds, the angels were glorious. The appearance of the messenger, the praise of the host of angels- they would have been overwhelmed with awe as they got a taste of what Heaven must be like.

The glory of Heaven here on earth was not dimmed by the Lord taking on the form of an infant. No, God was here with us, Emmanuel. Can we even fathom such a thing? Can we even for a moment take our thoughts away from the humbleness of His birth and see His glory? Can we, like the shepherds, drop everything for a while and run to where He is to see His glory for ourselves?

These special days of Advent have given us time to recognize all the other days we take His presence in our lives for granted. Caught up in our lives in this world with all the chores, errands, and appointments, with our responsibilities for our jobs, our families, our friends, and even our churches- don't we sometimes miss His glory? In fact, it's rare for us to take the time to let it wash over us and just stand for a moment in awe of Him. Our minds are always preoccupied, even in worship, with everything on our lengthy to-do lists so that the importance of the simple act of being with Him for no other purpose than enjoying His presence just never occurs to us.

The thing is, these moments of true worship are what our souls long for. Our hearts are restless and dissatisfied, our lives crave true fullness, because we were created for eternal life in the presence of God. He dwells with us today, but just imagine the glory we will experience when we are finally in His physical presence. It is in His presence that we can experience that peace the angels sang of and that Christ Himself promised.

Maybe today we can find the time to put aside the dangers and distractions of this life from our thoughts, and simply rest in the glory of our God, stand quietly in awe of Him for a little while, and just simply be with Him. In doing so, may we find the peace that only He can bring into our lives and our world.

# December 25, 2023

## CHRISTMAS DAY

The season of Advent and Christmas truly is all about Heaven. The joy, the peace, the hope, the love we experience are precious gifts we can enjoy every day- because of Jesus. I hope this book has brought you closer to Him this year. I hope your anticipation for Heaven has been rekindled and you have been comforted with these words that He is coming again.

I'm thankful today for the gift of the certainty that Heaven is my eternal home. Not everyone has that certainty. The truth is very simple- Jesus is the only way. He's done all the work for your redemption and He offers each of us a gift of faith. If you need to be certain your future is in Heaven, don't leave that offered gift under the tree. Just accept it today.

Today as we celebrate Christmas together with our families and friends, we can't help but remember the ones who aren't with us. This year my church has watched as several of our dearly loved members have gone to Heaven. Far from being sad about this today, we want to rejoice for them. They are finally home. They are right where we all long to be. As you remember those you may have lost this year, I hope you reflect on the sweetness of the memories, and the sweetness of knowing they are celebrating in Glory in the presence of the Guest of Honor- Jesus Christ.

The poem for today is dedicated to the memory of those members of First Baptist Church, Perry, Georgia, who are celebrating their first Christmas in Heaven.

Mrs. Annabelle Lytle
Mrs. Annie Patterson
Mrs. Joyce Griffin
Mr. Stewart Bloodworth
Mrs. Virginia Nadeau
Mr. Keith Seamon
Mr. Bill Jones
Mrs. Katherine McGehee
Mrs. Gertie Bell
Mr. Henry Dawkins
Mr. Jimmy Connell
Mrs. Mary Crowe
Mrs. Sandra Hunt
Mr. James "Stump" Langston
Mr. Bill Loudermilk

Finally Home for Christmas

It seems like just yesterday they were here with us.

    Tearing festive paper and bows from gifts

    Sneaking tastes of turkey

    Eating too much pie.

We miss them.

    That place around the tree seems so cold

    That seat at the table is silent

    The house isn't the same without them today.

But today they are finally Home for Christmas, and don't you wonder what it's like?

Can't you imagine

    The awe in their eyes

    The love in their hearts

    The joy they can't contain, bubbling up in laughter?

Can you imagine

    The music

    The beauty

    The peace

    Undimmed by tears, or age, or sickness, or sorrow?

All the joy, love, and laughter they shared with us for a lifetime

Can't compare with a single moment in their new Home, in Heaven.

    They have received the promised gift

    It is well with their souls forever

    They are finally home for Christmas.

We miss them, but not for long.

Sooner than we can imagine, we will know what they know

The joy, the peace, the music, the love

Soon the promise will be ours, too.

It will be well with our souls forever.

We will finally be home for Christmas.

# *Notes*

It is never my intention to present the words of others as my own. There are many pastors, teachers, and authors who have influenced me, and I have attempted to credit everyone I've read or heard throughout my preparation and writing of this book in the notes below. Any failure to do so is purely unintentional.

I am indebted throughout to the following commentaries which provided insight during my period of Scripture research and study.

Henry, Matthew. *Matthew Henry's Concise Commentary on the Whole Bible.* Thomas Nelson Publishers: Nashville. 1997.

MacArthur, John. *The MacArthur Study Bible. New American Standard Bible. Updated Edition.* Nelson Bibles. 2006.

Rydelnik, Michael and Vanlaningham, Michael ed. *The Moody Bible Commentary.* Moody Publishers: Chicago. 2014.

## OPENING LITURGY:

McElvey, Douglas. "A Liturgy to Mark the Start of the Christmas Season." *Every Moment Holy, Volume 1.* Rabbit Room Press: Nashville. 2019.

## WHERE HE DWELLS

Guiness, Os. Signals of Transcendence- Listening to the Promptings of Life. IVP: Downers Grove, IL. 2023.

Jeremiah, David. *Revealing the Mysteries of Heaven.* Turning Point for God: San Diego, CA. 2017.

## HOME FOR CHRISTMAS

"I'll Be Home for Christmas." Wikipedia. https://en.wikipedia.org/wiki/I%27ll_Be_Home_for_Christmas

Jeremiah, David. *Revealing the Mysteries of Heaven.* Turning Point for God: San Diego, CA. 2017.

## THE GOSPEL COMES WITH A HOUSE KEY

Butterfield, Rosaria. *The Gospel Comes with a House Key."* Crossway: Wheaton, IL. 2018.

## FINE LIVING

You can find Linda Smith Davis at https://newenglandfineliving.com

## POSSUM TROT, TEXAS

"Effective Compassion: Pure and faultless religion- S4. E10." 24 June 2023. https://wng.org/podcasts/effective-compassion-pure-and-faultless-religion-s4-e10-1687523478

Find more information about the CarePortal and the Global Orphan Project here: https://goproject.org

## THE LIST

"The Naughty and Nice List 2022." https://www.christmasaffairs.com/list/index.html

7 things you can't do in heaven, sermon by Louie Giglio, https://www.youtube.com/watch?v=_MvTcR4IvDw

Wendell Kimbrough's has written and recorded a song titled "You Belong" based on Psalm 87. He's worth looking up on social media. Website: https://www.wendellk.com

## FINDING MY PLACE

"Ches McCartney." Wikipedia. https://en.wikipedia.org/wiki/Ches_McCartney

## WHAT'S LEFT

Banks, Carter (BigBankz), "Exploring and Abandoned Christmas House," posted 24 December 2022, https://www.youtube.com/watch?v=dI8BrZsM6WI

## SOJOURNERS

Elrod, Brandon. "Send Relief, World Relief Working together to resettle Afghan refugees." North American Mission Board. 19 August 2021. https://www.namb.net/news/send-relief-world-relief-working-together-to-resettle-afghan-refugees/

Nelson, Jill. "Seeking a savior." WORLD Magazine. 9 March 2023. https://wng.org/articles/seeking-a-savior-1678156456

## STIRRING THE GUMBO

Jeremiah, David. *Revealing the Mysteries of Heaven*. Turning Point for God: San Diego, CA. 2017.

## THE GIFT OF THE (OTHER) MAGI

MacArthur, John. *The MacArthur Study Bible. New American Standard Bible. Updated Edition*. Nelson Bibles. 2006.

## THE ROYAL STANDARD

"The Royal Standard." https://www.royal.uk/encyclopedia/royal-standard

"Death and state funeral of Elizabeth II." Wikipedia. https://en.wikipedia.org/wiki/Death_and_state_funeral_of_Elizabeth_II

## YOUR TRUE FRIENDS

T.S. Eliot. "Choruses from the Rock" *The Complete Poems and Plays 1909-1950*. Harcourt Brace: Orlando. 1980

Smith, Joanne Huist. *The 13th Gift: A true story of a Christmas miracle*. Crown Publishing: New York. 2014.

## THE GRINCH

Witter, Brad. Who Was Dr. Seuss' Inspiration for the Grinch? Himself! https://www.biography.com/authors-writers/dr-seuss-grinch-inspiration. December 2020

## THE REJECTS

Vanlaningham, Michael G., "Matthew." *Moody Bible Commentary*. Moody Publishers: Chicago. 2014.

Henry, Matthew. *Matthew Henry's Concise Commentary on the Whole Bible*. Thomas Nelson Publishers: Nashville. 1997.

## LET THE STABLE STILL ASTONISH

Fields, Leslie Leyland, "Let the Stable Still Astonish" www.leslieleylandfields.com

"Love Letters from Jesus- Part 7. Our Spiritual Temperature." Jim Cymbala, Sermon from August 13, 2023. The Brooklyn Tabernacle.

https://media.brooklyntabernacle.org/sunday_media.html?_gl=
1*5fqssb*_ga*MTQxMjYzMTI5NS4xNjkyNDQyNjk1*_ga_TMT
P8WZQ0C*MTY5MjQ0MjY5NC4xLjAuMTY5MjQ0MjcwMC4wLj
AuMA..

# About the Author

Chrissie Tomlinson is a Bible teacher, a speaker, and the author of the inspirational blog, *ThisRoadHome*.com. She is also employed as a contracting officer for the Department of Defense.

She is the author of seven books (Available on Amazon):

*Advent to Advent*
*The Wondrous Gift*
*Glory: Rescued, Redeemed, Transformed*
*Journey of Hope*
*Not Fit to Eat: Dishes and Thoughts from a Vintage Southern Kitchen.*
*Adorned for Eternity*
*Soul Anchors (*only available from the author. Seriously- don't buy this one from Amazon).

She resides in Perry, Georgia. You can contact her at thisroadhomeblog@gmail.com.